D0007812

simply

pasta

simply
pasta

100 no fuss recipes for everyday cooking

First published in 2011

LOVE FOOD is an imprint of Parragon Books Ltd
Parragon
Queen Street House
4 Queen Street
Bath BA1 1HE, UK

Copyright © Parragon Books Ltd 2011

LOVE FOOD and the accompanying heart device is a registered
trademark of Parragon Books Ltd in Australia, the UK, USA, India,
and the EU.

www.parragon.com

All rights reserved. No part of this publication may be reproduced,
stored in a retrieval system, or transmitted, in any form or by any
means, electronic, mechanical, photocopying, recording, or
otherwise, without the prior permission of the copyright holder.

ISBN: 978-1-4454-5410-8

Printed in China

Introduction by Linda Doeser
New recipes by Teresa Goldfinch
Cover photography by Clive Streeter
Additional photography by Clive Bozzard-Hill
Cover food styling by Teresa Goldfinch
Additional food styling by Valerie Barrett

This book uses imperial, metric, and US cup measurements. Follow
the same units of measurement throughout; do not mix imperial and
metric. All spoon measurements are level: teaspoons are assumed
to be 5 ml, and tablespoons are assumed to be 15 ml. Unless
otherwise stated, milk is assumed to be whole, eggs are large,
individual vegetables, such as potatoes, are medium, and pepper is
freshly ground black pepper.

The times given are an approximate guide only. Preparation times
differ according to the techniques used by different people and
the cooking times may also vary from those given as a result of
the type of oven used. Optional ingredients, variations, or serving
suggestions have not been included in the calculations.

Recipes using raw or very lightly cooked eggs should be avoided
by infants, the elderly, pregnant women, convalescents, and anyone
with a chronic condition. Pregnant and breast-feeding women are
advised to avoid eating peanuts and peanut products. People with
nut allergies should be aware that some of the prepared
ingredients used in the recipes in this book may contain nuts.
Always check the packaging before use.

Vegetarians should be aware that some of the prepared
ingredients used in the recipes in this book may contain animal
products. Always check the packaging before use.

Contents

Introduction

Never mind the paintings of Leonardo da Vinci, the music of Giuseppe Verdi, or the poetry of Dante Alighieri, Italy's greatest gift to the world is undoubtedly pasta. Child or adult, virtually everybody loves it. It's quick and easy to cook. It goes with just about every other ingredient imaginable, so its versatility is almost endless. It's inexpensive and can be stored for a long time and is both filling and nourishing. It has existed since the days of the Roman Empire and is now eaten in every corner of the globe.

Pasta sauces can be made with meat, poultry, fish, shellfish, vegetables, mushrooms, cheese, and cream in just about any combination. At its simplest, it can be served with just garlic, olive oil, and parsley—a classic Roman dish that is surprisingly delicious. It can be layered with other ingredients and baked, or tubes can be stuffed and baked in a cream or tomato sauce. It may be served cold in salads or can provide the final flourish to homemade soups.

There are at least 200 pasta shapes—with about three times as many names, because they vary from region to region—and new "designer" shapes are constantly being added. Many have delightfully descriptive names that reflect their appearance, such as *ditali* "little thimbles," *penne* "quills," *farfalle* "butterflies," and *conchiglie* "shells." The origins of some other names, such as *strozzapreti* "priest stranglers," are more colorful; in this case, the legend of a gluttonous priest who nearly choked as a result of stuffing too much pasta into his mouth.

There are no rigid rules about which pasta to serve with which sauce, although some are traditional partners—tagliatelle with ragù or Bolognese sauce, linguine with clam sauce, and trenette with pesto, for example. As a general guide, long pasta, such as spaghetti, is best served with sauces based on olive oil so that the strands stay separate. Ribbons and medium-size tubular pasta go well with sauces based on butter, cream, and cheese, or on vegetables. Shapes, such as shells, are also good with vegetable sauces. Large penne, conchiglie, and rigatoni are good for baked dishes.

The best fresh pasta is made with eggs and flour. However, in some regions of Italy, water is substituted for some or all of the eggs, while commercially made dried pasta is made with durum wheat semolina and water. Pasta may be colored by adding spinach, tomatoes, saffron, or mushrooms to the dough to produce green, red, yellow, and brown pasta respectively.

Top Tips for Success

• All commercially made pasta is governed by strict laws but it is not all the same quality. The best, and so the more expensive, is dried for up to 80 hours, rather than the more usual 32.

• You need plenty of water in a large pan to boil pasta: allow about 4½ quarts for every 11–14 oz/300–400 g pasta. When the water comes to a boil, stir in the salt: add 3 tablespoons for this quantity. This sounds like a lot but it prevents the pasta from sticking together and very little, if any, is actually absorbed. When the salted water is at a rolling boil, add the pasta and immediately stir. Bring back to a boil before starting to count the cooking time and continue to boil—not simmer—until it is *al dente* (tender but still firm to the bite). Drain in a colander or remove strands with a long fork or spaghetti server.

• Cooking times vary depending on the shape and quality of the pasta, as well as whether it is fresh or dried. General guidelines are as follows: fresh, unfilled pasta 2–3 minutes; fresh, filled pasta 4–5 minutes; dried, unfilled pasta 8–12 minutes; dried, filled pasta 15–20 minutes.

• To test whether pasta is *al dente*, lift out a small piece and bite it between your front teeth. Start doing this a couple of minutes before the end of the recommended cooking time.

• Do not let cooked pasta stand around. Transfer it immediately to a warmed serving dish, add the sauce, and toss with two forks. Sometimes a little cooking water is added if the finished dish seems too dry. This is a fairly standard practice with fresh pasta, which absorbs more liquid.

• When pasta is cooked for salads, it can be treated in various ways, such as rinsing in hot water or refreshing under cold running water and tossing with olive oil or vinaigrette. However, do not just let it stand in the colander.

• Use tiny pasta shapes when you are cooking soup. These not only look attractive, but tend to stay on the diners' soup spoons more easily than larger pasta.

Sensational Soups & Salads

fresh tomato soup

SERVES 4

1 tbsp olive oil

10 plum tomatoes

1 onion, cut into quarters

1 garlic clove, thinly sliced

1 celery stalk, coarsely chopped

generous 2 cups chicken stock

2 oz/55 g dried anellini or other soup pasta

salt and pepper

chopped fresh flat-leaf parsley, to garnish

1 Heat the oil in a large, heavy-bottom pan and add the tomatoes, onion, garlic, and celery. Cover and cook over low heat for 45 minutes, occasionally shaking the pan gently, until the mixture is pulpy.

2 Transfer the mixture to a food processor or blender and process to a smooth puree. Push the puree through a strainer into a clean pan.

3 Add the stock and bring to a boil. Add the pasta, return to a boil, and cook for 8–10 minutes, or until the pasta is tender but still firm to the bite. Season to taste with salt and pepper. Ladle into warmed serving bowls, garnish with the parsley, and serve immediately.

tuscan bean soup

SERVES 6

10½ oz/300 g of canned cannellini beans, drained and rinsed

10½ oz/300 g of canned cranberry beans, drained and rinsed

about 2½ cups chicken or vegetable stock

4 oz/115 g dried macaroni

4–5 tbsp olive oil

2 garlic cloves, very finely chopped

3 tbsp chopped fresh flat-leaf parsley

salt and pepper

1 Place half of the cannellini and half of the cranberry beans in a food processor or blender with half of the stock and process until smooth. Pour into a large, heavy-bottom pan and add the remaining beans. Stir in enough of the remaining stock to achieve the consistency you like, then bring to a boil.

2 Add the pasta and return to a boil, then reduce the heat and cook for 8–10 minutes, or until tender but still firm to the bite.

3 Meanwhile, heat 3 tablespoons of the oil in a small skillet. Add the garlic and cook, stirring continuously, for 2–3 minutes, or until golden. Stir the garlic into the soup with the parsley.

4 Season to taste with salt and pepper and ladle into warmed serving bowls. Drizzle with the remaining olive oil to taste and serve immediately.

italian chicken soup

SERVES 4

1 lb/450 g skinless, boneless chicken breasts, cut into thin strips

5 cups chicken stock

⅔ cup heavy cream

4 oz/115 g dried vermicelli

1 tbsp cornstarch

3 tbsp milk

6 oz/175 g of canned corn kernels, drained

salt and pepper

1 Place the chicken in a large pan and pour in the chicken stock and cream. Bring to a boil, then reduce the heat and let simmer for 20 minutes.

2 Meanwhile, bring a large, heavy-bottom pan of lightly salted water to a boil. Add the pasta, return to a boil, and cook for 8–10 minutes, or until tender but still firm to the bite. Drain the pasta well and keep warm.

3 Season the soup to taste with salt and pepper. Mix the cornstarch and milk together until a smooth paste forms, then stir it into the soup. Add the corn and pasta and heat through. Ladle into warmed serving bowls and serve immediately.

hearty bean & pasta soup

SERVES 4

4 tbsp olive oil

1 onion, finely chopped

1 celery stalk, chopped

1 carrot, diced

1 bay leaf

5 cups vegetable stock

14 oz/400 g of canned chopped tomatoes

6 oz/175 g dried pasta shapes, such as farfalle, shells, or twists

14 oz/400 g of canned cannellini beans, drained and rinsed

3½ cups shredded spinach or Swiss chard (thick stems removed)

salt and pepper

⅓ cup finely grated Parmesan cheese, to serve

1 Heat the olive oil in a large, heavy-bottom pan. Add the onion, celery, and carrot and cook over medium heat for 8–10 minutes, stirring occasionally, until the vegetables slightly soften. Add the bay leaf, stock, and tomatoes, then bring to a boil.

2 Reduce the heat, cover, and simmer for 15 minutes, or until the vegetables are just tender. Add the pasta and beans, then bring the soup back to a boil and cook for 10 minutes, until the pasta is tender but still firm to the bite.

3 Stir occasionally to prevent the pasta from sticking to the bottom of the pan and burning. Season to taste with salt and pepper, add the spinach, and cook for an additional 2 minutes, or until tender. Ladle the soup into warmed bowls and serve with Parmesan cheese.

Step 1

Step 1

Step 2

potato & pesto soup

SERVES 4

2 tbsp olive oil

3 strips smoked bacon, chopped

2 tbsp butter

4 potatoes, finely chopped

4 onions, finely chopped

2½ cups chicken stock

2½ cups milk

3½ oz/100 g dried conchigliette (small pasta shells)

⅔ cup heavy cream

2 tbsp pesto

2 tbsp chopped fresh flat-leaf parsley

salt and pepper

shavings of fresh Parmesan, to serve

1 Heat the oil in a large saucepan and cook the bacon over medium heat for 4 minutes. Add the butter, potatoes, and onions, and cook for 12 minutes, stirring continuously.

2 Add the stock and milk to the pan, bring to a boil, and simmer for 5 minutes. Add the pasta and simmer for an additional 3–5 minutes.

3 Blend in the cream and simmer for 5 minutes. Add the pesto and chopped parsley and season to taste with salt and pepper. Transfer the soup to warmed serving bowls and serve with Parmesan cheese.

minestrone

SERVES 4

2 tbsp olive oil

2 garlic cloves, chopped

2 red onions, chopped

2¾ oz/75 g prosciutto, sliced

1 red bell pepper, seeded and chopped

1 orange bell pepper, seeded and chopped

14 oz/400 g of canned chopped tomatoes

4 cups vegetable stock

1 celery stalk, chopped

14 oz/400 g of canned cranberry beans, drained and rinsed

1 cup shredded green or white cabbage

½ cup frozen peas, thawed

1 tbsp chopped fresh flat-leaf parsley

2¾ oz/75 g dried vermicelli

salt and pepper

freshly grated Parmesan cheese, to garnish

1 Heat the oil in a large pan. Add the garlic, onions, and prosciutto and cook over medium heat, stirring, for 3 minutes, until slightly softened. Add the red and orange bell peppers and the chopped tomatoes, and cook for an additional 2 minutes, stirring.

2 Stir in the stock, then add the celery, cranberry beans, cabbage, peas, and parsley. Season to taste with salt and pepper. Bring to a boil, then lower the heat and simmer for 30 minutes.

3 Add the vermicelli to the pan. Cook for another 4–5 minutes, or until the pasta is tender but still firm to the bite. Remove from the heat and ladle into warmed serving bowls. Garnish with freshly grated Parmesan and serve immediately.

chicken & chickpea soup

SERVES 4

2 tbsp butter

3 scallions, chopped

2 garlic cloves, finely chopped

1 fresh marjoram sprig, finely chopped

12 oz/350 g skinless, boneless chicken breasts, diced

5 cups chicken stock

12 oz/350 g of canned chickpeas, drained and rinsed

1 bouquet garni

1 red bell pepper, seeded and diced

1 green bell pepper, seeded and diced

4 oz/115 g dried macaroni

salt and white pepper

croutons, to serve

1 Melt the butter in a large pan over medium heat. Add the scallions, garlic, marjoram, and chicken and cook, stirring frequently, for 5 minutes.

2 Add the stock, chickpeas, and bouquet garni, then season to taste with salt and white pepper. Bring the soup to a boil over medium heat, then reduce the heat and simmer for about 2 hours.

3 Add the diced bell peppers and pasta to the pan, then simmer for an additional 20 minutes. Ladle the soup into warmed serving bowls and sprinkle the croutons over the top. Serve immediately.

scallop soup
with pasta

SERVES 6

1 lb 2 oz/500 g shelled
sea scallops

1½ cups milk

7 cups vegetable stock

generous 1 cup frozen baby
peas

6 oz/175 g dried taglialini

5 tbsp butter

2 scallions, finely chopped

¾ cup dry white wine

3 slices prosciutto,
cut into thin strips

salt and pepper

chopped fresh flat-leaf
parsley, to garnish

1 Slice the sea scallops in half horizontally and season with salt and pepper.

2 Pour the milk and vegetable stock into a pan, add a pinch of salt, and bring to a boil. Add the peas and pasta, return to a boil, and cook for 8–10 minutes, or until the taglialini is tender but still firm to the bite.

3 Meanwhile, melt the butter in a skillet. Add the scallions and cook over low heat, stirring occasionally, for 3 minutes. Add the sea scallops and cook for 45 seconds on each side. Pour in the wine, add the prosciutto, and cook for 2–3 minutes.

4 Stir the sea scallop mixture into the soup, taste, and adjust the seasoning, if necessary, and garnish with the parsley. Serve immediately.

Step 1

Step 2

Step 4

fish soup with macaroni

SERVES 6

2 tbsp olive oil

2 onions, sliced

1 garlic clove, finely chopped

4 cups fish stock or water

14 oz/400 g of canned chopped tomatoes

¼ tsp herbes de Provence

¼ tsp saffron threads

4 oz/115 g dried macaroni

18 mussels, scrubbed and debearded

1 lb/450 g monkfish fillet, skinned and cut into chunks

8 oz/225 g raw shrimp, peeled and deveined, tails left on

salt and pepper

1 Heat the oil in a large, heavy-bottom pan. Add the onions and garlic and cook over low heat, stirring occasionally, for 5 minutes, or until the onions have softened.

2 Add the stock with the tomatoes and their can juices, herbs, saffron, and pasta, and season to taste with salt and pepper. Bring to a boil, then cover and simmer for 15 minutes.

3 Discard any mussels with broken shells or any that refuse to close when tapped. Add the mussels, monkfish, and shrimp to the pan. Re-cover and simmer for an additional 5–10 minutes, until the mussels have opened, the shrimp have changed color, and the fish is opaque and flakes easily. Discard any mussels that remain closed. Ladle the soup into warmed serving bowls and serve immediately.

brown lentil & pasta soup

SERVES 4

**4 strips lean bacon,
cut into small squares**

1 onion, chopped

2 garlic cloves, crushed

2 celery stalks, chopped

**1¾ oz/50 g dried farfallini
(small pasta bows)**

**14 oz/400 g of canned
brown lentils, drained
and rinsed**

5 cups vegetable stock

**2 tbsp chopped fresh mint,
plus extra sprigs
to garnish**

1 Place the bacon in a large skillet together with the onion, garlic, and celery. Cook for 4–5 minutes, stirring, until the onion is tender and the bacon is just beginning to brown.

2 Add the pasta to the skillet and cook, stirring, for 1 minute to coat the pasta in the fat.

3 Add the lentils and the stock, and bring to a boil. Reduce the heat and simmer for 8–10 minutes, or until the pasta is tender but still firm to the bite.

4 Remove the skillet from the heat and stir in the chopped fresh mint. Transfer to warmed serving bowls, garnish with fresh mint sprigs, and serve immediately.

tuscan veal broth

SERVES 4

⅓ cup dried peas, soaked for 2 hours and drained

2 lb/900 g boned neck of veal, diced

5 cups beef stock

2½ cups water

⅓ cup pearl barley, washed

1 large carrot, diced

1 small turnip (about 6 oz/175 g), diced

1 large leek, thinly sliced

1 red onion, finely chopped

½ cup chopped tomatoes

1 fresh basil sprig

3½ oz/100 g dried vermicelli

salt and pepper

1 Put the peas, veal, stock, and water into a large pan and bring to a boil over low heat. Using a slotted spoon, skim off any foam that rises to the surface.

2 When all of the foam has been removed, add the pearl barley and a pinch of salt to the mixture. Simmer gently over low heat for 25 minutes.

3 Add the carrot, turnip, leek, onion, tomatoes, and basil to the pan, and season to taste with salt and pepper. Simmer for about 2 hours, skimming the surface from time to time to remove any foam. Remove the pan from the heat and set aside for 2 hours.

4 Set the pan over medium heat and bring to a boil. Add the vermicelli and cook for 8–10 minutes. Season to taste with salt and pepper, then remove and discard the basil. Ladle into warmed serving bowls and serve.

chicken, bacon & avocado salad

SERVES 2

5½ oz/150 g dried farfalle

2 thick strips smoked bacon

7 oz/200 g cooked skinless, boneless chicken breasts, sliced

2 plum tomatoes, sliced

1 large avocado, halved, pitted, and sliced

¼ cup arugula

salt

dressing

6 tbsp olive oil

3 tbsp lemon juice

1 tsp Dijon mustard

1–2 garlic cloves, crushed

salt and pepper

1 Bring a large, heavy-bottom pan of lightly salted water to a boil. Add the pasta, return to a boil, and cook for 8–10 minutes, or until tender but still firm to the bite. Meanwhile put all the ingredients for the dressing in a screw-top jar, seasoning well with salt and pepper. Screw the lid on tightly and shake well to combine.

2 When the pasta is cooked, drain and transfer to a large bowl. Add half of the dressing, then toss together and let cool. Preheat the broiler to high.

3 Broil the bacon for 2–3 minutes, turning until crispy. Transfer the bacon to a cutting board and slice into chunky pieces. Add the pieces to the bowl of pasta with the chicken, tomatoes, avocado, and arugula. Pour the remaining dressing over the top and toss well. Serve immediately.

Step 1

Step 2

Step 3

tuna & herbed fusilli salad

SERVES 4

7 oz/200 g dried fusilli

1 red bell pepper, seeded and quartered

1 red onion, sliced

4 tomatoes, sliced

7 oz/200 g of canned tuna in brine, drained and flaked

salt

dressing

6 tbsp basil-flavored oil or extra virgin olive oil

3 tbsp white wine vinegar

1 tbsp lime juice

1 tsp mustard

1 tsp honey

4 tbsp chopped fresh basil, plus extra sprigs to garnish

1 Bring a large, heavy-bottom pan of lightly salted water to a boil. Add the pasta, return to a boil, and cook for 8–10 minutes, or until tender but still firm to the bite.

2 Meanwhile, put the bell pepper quarters under a preheated hot broiler and broil for 10–12 minutes, or until the skins begin to blacken. Transfer to a plastic bag, seal, and set aside.

3 Remove the pasta from the heat, drain, and set aside to cool. Remove the bell pepper quarters from the bag and peel off the skins. Slice the bell pepper into strips.

4 To make the dressing, put all the dressing ingredients in a large bowl and stir together well. Add the pasta, bell pepper strips, onion, tomatoes, and tuna. Toss together gently, garnish with basil springs, and serve.

pasta salad with bell peppers

SERVES 4

1 red bell pepper

1 orange bell pepper

10 oz/280 g dried conchiglie (shells)

5 tbsp extra virgin olive oil

2 tbsp lemon juice

2 tbsp pesto

1 garlic clove, very finely chopped

3 tbsp shredded fresh basil leaves

salt and pepper

1 Put the whole bell peppers on a baking sheet and place under a preheated broiler, turning frequently, for 15 minutes, until charred all over. Remove with tongs and place in a bowl. Cover with crumpled paper towels and set aside.

2 Meanwhile, bring a large, heavy-bottom pan of lightly salted water to a boil. Add the pasta, return to a boil, and cook for 8–10 minutes, or until tender but still firm to the bite.

3 Combine the olive oil, lemon juice, pesto, and garlic in a bowl, whisking well to mix. Drain the pasta, add it to the pesto mixture while still hot, and toss well. Set aside.

4 When the bell peppers are cool enough to handle, peel off the skins, then cut open and remove the seeds. Chop the flesh coarsely and add to the pasta with the basil. Season to taste with salt and pepper and toss well. Serve at room temperature.

warm pasta salad

SERVES 4

8 oz/225 g dried farfalle

**6 pieces of sun-dried
tomato in oil, drained
and chopped**

4 scallions, chopped

1¼ cups arugula, shredded

**½ cucumber, seeded and
diced**

salt and pepper

**freshly grated Parmesan
cheese, to serve**

dressing

4 tbsp olive oil

1 tbsp white wine vinegar

½ tsp superfine sugar

1 tsp whole grain mustard

**4 fresh basil leaves,
finely shredded**

salt and pepper

1 To make the dressing, whisk the oil, vinegar, sugar, and mustard together in a bowl or pitcher. Season to taste with salt and pepper and stir in the basil.

2 Bring a large, heavy-bottom pan of lightly salted water to a boil. Add the pasta, return to a boil, and cook for 8–10 minutes, or until tender but still firm to the bite. Drain and transfer to a salad bowl. Add the dressing and toss well.

3 Add the tomatoes, scallions, arugula, and cucumber, season to taste with salt and pepper, and toss. Sprinkle with the Parmesan cheese and serve warm.

tomato, olive & mozzarella pasta salad

SERVES 4

8 oz/225 g dried conchiglie (shells)

⅓ cup pine nuts

2½ cups halved cherry tomatoes

1 red bell pepper, seeded and cut into bite-size chunks

1 red onion, chopped

7 oz/200 g buffalo mozzarella, cut into small pieces

12 black olives, pitted

1 cup fresh basil leaves

fresh Parmesan cheese shavings, to garnish

salt

dressing

5 tbsp extra virgin olive oil

2 tbsp balsamic vinegar

1 tbsp chopped fresh basil

salt and pepper

1 Bring a large, heavy-bottom pan of lightly salted water to a boil. Add the pasta, return to a boil, and cook for 8–10 minutes, or until tender but still firm to the bite. Drain, refresh under cold running water, and drain again. Let cool.

2 Meanwhile, heat a dry skillet over low heat, add the pine nuts, and cook, shaking the skillet frequently, for 1–2 minutes, or until lightly toasted. Remove from the heat, transfer to a dish, and let cool.

3 To make the dressing, put all the ingredients in a small bowl and mix together well. Season to taste with salt and pepper. Cover with plastic wrap, and set aside.

4 To assemble the salad, divide the pasta among four serving bowls. Add the pine nuts, tomatoes, bell pepper, onion, mozzarella, and olives to each bowl. Sprinkle the basil over the top, then drizzle with the dressing. Garnish with Parmesan cheese shavings and serve.

Step 2

Step 3

Step 4

neapolitan seafood salad

SERVES 4

1 lb/450 g prepared squid, cut into strips

1 lb 10 oz/750 g cooked mussels

1 lb/450 g cooked baby clams in brine, drained

½ cup dry white wine

1½ cups olive oil

6 oz/175 g dried orecchiette (pasta shells)

juice of 1 lemon

1 bunch fresh chives, snipped

1 bunch fresh flat-leaf parsley, finely chopped

mixed salad greens

4 large tomatoes, quartered

salt and pepper

1 Put all of the seafood into a large bowl. Pour in the wine and half of the olive oil, then set aside for 6 hours.

2 Put the seafood mixture into a pan and simmer over low heat for 10 minutes. Set aside to cool.

3 Bring a large, heavy-bottom pan of lightly salted water to a boil. Add the pasta and 1 tablespoon of the remaining olive oil, return to a boil, and cook for 8–10 minutes, or until tender but still firm to the bite. Drain thoroughly and refresh in cold water.

4 Strain off about half of the cooking liquid from the seafood and discard the rest. Mix in the lemon juice, chives, parsley, and the remaining olive oil. Season to taste with salt and pepper. Drain the pasta and add to the seafood.

5 Shred the salad leaves and arrange them in the bottom of a salad bowl. Spoon the seafood salad into the bowl, top with the tomatoes, and serve.

spicy sausage pasta salad

SERVES 4

4½ oz/125 g dried conchiglie (shells)

2 tbsp olive oil

1 onion, chopped

2 garlic cloves, very finely chopped

1 small yellow bell pepper, seeded and cut into very thin sticks

6 oz/175 g spicy pork sausage, such as chorizo, pepperoni, or salami, skinned and sliced

2 tbsp red wine

1 tbsp red wine vinegar

4½ oz/125 g mixed salad greens

salt

1 Bring a large, heavy-bottom pan of lightly salted water to a boil. Add the pasta, return to a boil, and cook for 8–10 minutes, or until tender but still firm to the bite. Drain and set aside.

2 Heat the oil in a pan over medium heat. Add the onion and cook until translucent, then stir in the garlic, yellow bell pepper, and sausage, and cook for 3–4 minutes, stirring once or twice.

3 Add the wine, vinegar, and reserved pasta to the pan, stir, and bring the mixture just to a boil over medium heat.

4 Arrange the salad greens on serving plates, spoon the warm sausage and pasta mixture over the top, and serve immediately.

penne & apple salad

SERVES 4

2 large heads of lettuce

9 oz/250 g dried penne

1 tbsp olive oil

8 red apples, such as Lady Apples

juice of 4 lemons

1 stalk of celery, sliced

¾ cup walnut halves

1 cup fresh garlic mayonnaise

salt

1 Wash and drain the lettuce leaves, then pat them dry with paper towels. Transfer them to the refrigerator for 1 hour, until crisp.

2 Meanwhile, bring a large, heavy-bottom pan of lightly salted water to a boil. Add the pasta and olive oil, return to a boil, and cook for 8–10 minutes, or until tender but still firm to the bite. Drain the pasta and refresh under cold running water. Drain thoroughly and set aside.

3 Core and dice the apples, then place them in a small bowl and sprinkle with the lemon juice to coat them thoroughly—this will prevent them from turning brown. Mix together the pasta, celery, apples, and walnut halves and toss the mixture in the garlic mayonnaise. Add more mayonnaise, to taste.

4 Line a salad bowl with the lettuce leaves and spoon the pasta salad into the lined bowl. Refrigerate until ready to serve.

honey & chicken pasta salad

SERVES 4

9 oz/250 g dried pasta twirls, such as fusilli

2 tbsp olive oil

1 onion, thinly sliced

1 garlic clove, crushed

14 oz/400 g skinless, boneless chicken breasts, thinly sliced

2 tbsp whole grain mustard

2 tbsp honey

10 cherry tomatoes, halved

handful of mizuna or arugula leaves

fresh thyme leaves, to garnish

salt

dressing

3 tbsp olive oil

1 tbsp sherry vinegar

2 tsp honey

1 tbsp fresh thyme leaves

salt and pepper

1 To make the dressing, whisk the dressing ingredients together in a bowl. Season to taste with salt and pepper.

2 Bring a large, heavy-bottom pan of lightly salted water to a boil. Add the pasta, return to a boil, and cook for 8–10 minutes, or until tender but still firm to the bite.

3 Meanwhile, heat the oil in a large skillet. Add the onion and garlic and cook for 5 minutes. Add the chicken and cook, stirring frequently, for 3–4 minutes, or until just cooked through. Stir the mustard and honey into the pan and cook for another 2–3 minutes, or until the chicken and onion are golden brown and sticky.

4 Drain the pasta and transfer to a serving bowl. Pour the dressing over it and toss well. Stir in the chicken and onion and let cool.

5 Gently stir the tomatoes and mizuna into the pasta. Serve garnished with the thyme leaves.

Step 1

Step 3

Step 3

rare beef pasta salad

SERVES 4

1 lb/450 g sirloin or porterhouse steak in 1 piece

1 lb/450 g dried fusilli

4 tbsp olive oil

2 tbsp lime juice

2 tbsp Thai fish sauce

2 tsp honey

4 scallions, sliced

1 cucumber, peeled and cut into 1-inch/2.5-cm chunks

3 tomatoes, cut into wedges

1 tbsp finely chopped fresh mint

salt and pepper

1 Season the steak with salt and pepper. Preheat the broiler to high, then broil the steak for about 4 minutes on each side. Let stand for 5 minutes, then slice thinly across the grain.

2 Meanwhile, bring a large, heavy-bottom pan of lightly salted water to a boil. Add the pasta, return to a boil, and cook for 8–10 minutes, or until tender but still firm to the bite. Drain the pasta thoroughly, then refresh in cold water and drain again. Return the pasta to the pan and toss in the oil.

3 Mix the lime juice, fish sauce, and honey together in a small pan and cook over medium heat for about 2 minutes.

4 Add the scallions, cucumber, tomatoes, and chopped mint to the pan, then add the steak and mix well. Season with salt and pepper to taste.

5 Transfer the pasta to a large, warmed serving dish and top with the steak mixture. Serve just warm or let cool completely.

pasta salad with melon & shrimp

SERVES 6

8 oz/225 g dried green fusilli

5 tbsp extra virgin olive oil

1 lb/450 g cooked shrimp

1 cantaloupe melon

1 honeydew melon

1 tbsp red wine vinegar

1 tsp whole grain mustard

pinch of superfine sugar

1 tbsp chopped fresh flat-leaf parsley

1 tbsp chopped fresh basil, plus extra sprigs to garnish

1 oak leaf lettuce, shredded

salt and pepper

1 Bring a large, heavy-bottom pan of lightly salted water to a boil. Add the pasta, return to a boil, and cook for 8–10 minutes, or until tender but still firm to the bite. Drain, toss with 1 tablespoon of the olive oil, and let cool.

2 Meanwhile, place the shrimp in a large bowl. Halve both of the melons and scoop out the seeds with a spoon. Using a melon baller or teaspoon, scoop out balls of the flesh and add them to the shrimp.

3 Whisk together the remaining olive oil, the vinegar, mustard, sugar, parsley, and basil in a small bowl. Season to taste with salt and pepper. Add the cooled pasta to the shrimp and melon mixture and toss lightly to mix, then pour in the dressing, and toss again. Cover with plastic wrap and chill in the refrigerator for 30 minutes.

4 Make a bed of shredded lettuce on a serving plate. Spoon the pasta salad on top, garnish with basil leaves, and serve.

niçoise pasta salad

SERVES 4

12 oz/350 g dried conchiglie (shells)

1 cup green beans

1¾ oz/50 g of canned anchovy fillets, drained

2 tbsp milk

2 small heads of crisp lettuce

3 large tomatoes

4 hard-boiled eggs

8 oz/225 g of canned tuna, drained

1 cup pitted ripe black olives

salt

vinaigrette dressing

¼ cup extra virgin olive oil

2 tbsp white wine vinegar

1 tsp whole grain mustard

salt and pepper

1 Bring a large, heavy-bottom pan of lightly salted water to a boil. Add the pasta, return to a boil, and cook for 8–10 minutes, or until tender but still firm to the bite. Drain the pasta thoroughly and refresh in cold water.

2 Bring a small pan of lightly salted water to a boil over medium heat. Add the beans and cook for 10–12 minutes, or until softened. Drain thoroughly and refresh in cold water, then drain again and set aside.

3 Put the anchovies into a shallow bowl, then pour in the milk and set aside for 10 minutes. Meanwhile, tear the lettuce into large pieces. Blanch the tomatoes in boiling water for 1–2 minutes, then drain. Skin and coarsely chop the flesh. Shell the eggs and cut into quarters. Flake the tuna into large chunks.

4 Drain the anchovies and the pasta. Put the anchovies, pasta, beans, lettuce, tomatoes, eggs, tuna, and olives into a large bowl and gently mix together.

5 To make the vinaigrette dressing, beat the oil, vinegar, and mustard together, season to taste with salt and pepper, and keep in the refrigerator until ready to serve. Just before serving, pour the vinaigrette dressing over the salad.

pasta salad with walnuts & gorgonzola

SERVES 4

8 oz/225 g dried farfalle

2 tbsp walnut oil

4 tbsp safflower or sunflower oil

2 tbsp balsamic vinegar

10 oz/280 g mixed salad greens

8 oz/225 g Gorgonzola cheese, diced

½ cup walnuts, halved and toasted

salt and pepper

1 Bring a large, heavy-bottom pan of lightly salted water to a boil. Add the pasta, return to a boil, and cook for 8–10 minutes, or until tender but still firm to the bite. Drain and refresh in a bowl of cold water. Drain again.

2 Mix the walnut oil, safflower oil, and vinegar together in a bowl, whisking well, and season to taste with salt and pepper.

3 Arrange the salad greens in a large serving bowl. Top with the pasta, Gorgonzola cheese, and walnuts. Pour the dressing over the salad, toss lightly, and serve.

VARIATION
Replace the Gorgonzola cheese with ricotta to give the salad a milder cheese flavor.

2

Mouth-watering Meat & Poultry

spaghetti with meatballs

SERVES 6

1 potato, diced

14 oz/400 g ground beef

1 onion, finely chopped

1 egg

4 tbsp chopped fresh flat-leaf parsley

all-purpose flour, for dusting

5 tbsp olive oil

1¾ cups tomato puree

2 tbsp tomato paste

14 oz/400 g dried spaghetti

salt and pepper

fresh basil leaves, to garnish

shavings of fresh Parmesan cheese, to garnish

1 Place the potato in a small pan, add cold water to cover and a pinch of salt, and bring to a boil. Cook for 10–15 minutes, or until tender, then drain. Either mash thoroughly with a potato masher or fork or pass through a potato ricer.

2 Combine the potato, beef, onion, egg, and parsley in a bowl and season to taste with salt and pepper. Spread out the flour on a plate. With dampened hands, shape the meat mixture into walnut-size balls and roll in the flour. Shake off any excess.

3 Heat the olive oil in a heavy-bottom skillet, add the meatballs, and cook over medium heat, stirring and turning frequently, for 8–10 minutes, or until golden all over. Add the tomato puree and tomato paste and cook for an additional 10 minutes, or until the sauce is reduced and thickened.

4 Meanwhile, bring a large, heavy-bottom pan of lightly salted water to a boil. Add the pasta, return to a boil, and cook for 8–10 minutes, or until tender but still firm to the bite.

5 Drain well and add to the meatball sauce, tossing well to coat. Transfer to a warmed serving dish, garnish with the basil leaves and Parmesan cheese, and serve immediately.

spaghetti bolognese

SERVES 4

1 tbsp olive oil

1 onion, finely chopped

2 garlic cloves, chopped

1 carrot, chopped

1 celery stalk, chopped

1¾ oz/50 g pancetta or bacon, diced

12 oz/350 g lean ground beef

14 oz/400 g of canned chopped tomatoes

2 tsp dried oregano

½ cup red wine

2 tbsp tomato paste

12 oz/350 g dried spaghetti

salt and pepper

chopped fresh flat-leaf parsley, to garnish

1 Heat the oil in a large skillet. Add the onion and cook for 3 minutes. Add the garlic, carrot, celery, and pancetta and cook for 3–4 minutes, or until just beginning to brown.

2 Add the beef and cook over high heat for an additional 3 minutes, or until the meat has browned. Stir in the tomatoes, oregano, and red wine and bring to a boil. Reduce the heat and simmer for about 45 minutes.

3 Stir in the tomato paste and season to taste with salt and pepper.

4 Bring a large, heavy-bottom pan of lightly salted water to a boil. Add the pasta, return to a boil, and cook for 8–10 minutes, or until tender but still firm to the bite. Drain thoroughly.

5 Transfer the spaghetti to a warmed serving dish and pour the bolognese sauce over the top. Toss to mix well, garnish with parsley, and serve immediately.

linguine with bacon & olives

SERVES 4

3 tbsp olive oil

2 onions, thinly sliced

2 garlic cloves, finely chopped

6 oz/175 g rindless bacon, diced

3¼ cups sliced white mushrooms

5 canned anchovy fillets, drained

6 black olives, pitted and halved

1 lb/450 g dried linguine

¼ cup freshly grated Parmesan cheese

salt and pepper

1 Heat the olive oil in a large skillet. Add the onions, garlic, and bacon, and cook over low heat, stirring occasionally, until the onions are softened. Stir in the mushrooms, anchovies, and olives, then season to taste with salt and pepper. Simmer for 5 minutes.

2 Meanwhile, bring a large, heavy-bottom pan of lightly salted water to a boil. Add the pasta, return to a boil, and cook for 8–10 minutes, or until tender but still firm to the bite.

3 Drain the pasta and transfer to a warmed serving dish. Spoon the sauce on top, toss lightly, and sprinkle with the Parmesan cheese. Serve immediately.

spaghetti with bacon & crispy breadcrumbs

SERVES 2

2 oz/55 g day-old ciabatta bread (about 1 roll)

sprig of rosemary

6 oz/175 g dried spaghetti

2 tsp olive oil

5 oz/140 g smoked bacon, chopped

1 tbsp butter

⅓ cup pine nuts

2 garlic cloves, crushed

2–3 tbsp chopped fresh flat-leaf parsley

salt and pepper

1 Put the bread, including any crusts, into a food processor and process to make coarse breadcrumbs. Bruise the rosemary sprig in a pestle with a mortar or use a rolling pin to release the flavor.

2 Bring a large, heavy-bottom pan of lightly salted water to a boil. Add the pasta, return to a boil, and cook for 8–10 minutes, or until tender but still firm to the bite. Meanwhile, heat the oil in a large skillet, add the bacon and rosemary, and cook for 2–3 minutes, or until the bacon is golden brown. Transfer to a warmed serving bowl using a slotted spoon.

3 Add the butter to the bacon fat remaining in the skillet. When melted and foaming, add the breadcrumbs, pine nuts, and garlic. Cook for 2–3 minutes, stirring until golden brown, then tip into the bowl with the bacon.

4 Drain the pasta and transfer to the bowl with the bacon and breadcrumbs. Add the parsley, season with pepper, and toss well. Serve immediately.

Step 1

Step 2

Step 3

spaghetti alla carbonara

SERVES 4

1 lb/450 g dried spaghetti

1 tbsp olive oil

**8 oz/225 g rindless
pancetta or lean bacon,
chopped**

4 eggs

5 tbsp light cream

**2 tbsp freshly grated
Parmesan cheese**

salt and pepper

1 Bring a large, heavy-bottom pan of lightly salted water to a boil. Add the pasta, return to a boil, and cook for 8–10 minutes, or until tender but still firm to the bite.

2 Meanwhile, heat the oil in a heavy-bottom skillet. Add the pancetta and cook over medium heat, stirring frequently, for 8–10 minutes.

3 Beat the eggs with the cream in a small bowl and season to taste with salt and pepper. Drain the pasta and return it to the pan. Turn in the contents of the skillet, then add the egg mixture and half of the Parmesan cheese. Stir well, then transfer to a warmed serving dish. Serve immediately, sprinkled with the remaining cheese.

pasta with bacon & tomatoes

SERVES 4

10 small, sweet tomatoes (about 2 lb/900 g)

6 strips rindless smoked bacon

4 tbsp butter

1 onion, chopped

1 garlic clove, crushed

4 fresh oregano sprigs, finely chopped

1 lb/450 g dried orecchiette (pasta shells)

salt and pepper

freshly grated Romano cheese

1 Blanch the tomatoes in boiling water. Drain, peel, and seed the tomatoes, then coarsely chop the flesh.

2 Using a sharp knife, chop the bacon into small dice. Melt the butter in a pan. Add the bacon and cook until it is golden.

3 Add the onion and garlic, and cook over medium heat for 5–7 minutes, or until just softened. Add the tomatoes and oregano to the pan, then season to taste with salt and pepper. Lower the heat and simmer for 10–12 minutes.

4 Bring a large, heavy-bottom pan of lightly salted water to a boil. Add the pasta, return to a boil, and cook for 8–10 minutes, or until tender but still firm to the bite. Drain the pasta and transfer to a warmed serving dish.

5 Spoon the bacon and tomato sauce over the top of the pasta. Toss to coat, sprinkle with the Romano cheese, and serve immediately.

fusilli with bacon, eggs & mushrooms

SERVES 6

1 tbsp olive oil

4 strips lean bacon or pancetta

2 cups mushrooms, sliced

8 oz/225 g dried fusilli

2 eggs, beaten

4 oz/115 g cheddar or mozzarella cheese, diced

salt and pepper

chopped fresh flat-leaf parsley, to garnish

1 Heat the oil in a skillet over medium heat. Add the bacon and cook until crisp. Remove with tongs, cut into small pieces, and keep warm.

2 Cook the mushrooms in the skillet with the bacon fat for 5–7 minutes, or until softened. Remove from the heat.

3 Bring a large, heavy-bottom pan of lightly salted water to a boil. Add the pasta, return to a boil, and cook for 8–10 minutes, or until tender but still firm to the bite. Drain the pasta and return to the pan.

4 Stir the mushrooms, beaten eggs, and the cheese pieces into the pasta. Season with pepper and toss until the eggs have coated the pasta and the cheese has melted.

5 Transfer to a warmed serving dish. Sprinkle with the bacon pieces and parsley and serve immediately.

pork & pasta casserole

SERVES 4

2 tbsp olive oil

1 onion, chopped

1 garlic clove, finely chopped

2 carrots, diced

2 oz/55 g pancetta or lean bacon, chopped

1⅔ cups chopped white mushrooms

1 lb/450 g fresh ground pork

½ cup dry white wine

4 tbsp tomato puree

7 oz/200 g of canned chopped tomatoes

2 tsp chopped fresh sage

8 oz/225 g dried penne

5 oz/140 g mozzarella cheese, diced

¼ cup freshly grated Parmesan

1¼ cups prepared white sauce or Alfredo sauce

salt and pepper

1 Preheat the oven to 400°F/200°C. Heat the oil in a large, heavy-bottom skillet. Add the onion, garlic, and carrots and cook over low heat, stirring occasionally, for 5 minutes, or until the onion has softened.

2 Add the pancetta and cook for 5 minutes. Add the chopped mushrooms and cook, stirring occasionally, for an additional 2 minutes. Add the pork and cook until the meat is browned. Stir in the wine, tomato puree, tomatoes, and chopped fresh sage. Season to taste with salt and pepper, bring to a boil, then cover and simmer over low heat for 25–30 minutes.

3 Meanwhile, bring a large, heavy-bottom saucepan of lightly salted water to a boil. Add the pasta, return to a boil, and cook for 8–10 minutes, or until tender but still firm to the bite. Spoon the pork mixture into a large casserole dish. Stir the mozzarella cheese and half of the Parmesan cheese into the white sauce.

4 Drain the pasta and stir the cheese sauce into it, then spoon it over the pork mixture. Sprinkle with the remaining Parmesan cheese and bake in the preheated oven for 25–30 minutes, or until golden brown. Serve immediately.

Step 1

Step 2

Step 4

saffron & ham linguine

SERVES 4

12 oz/350 g dried linguine

pinch of saffron threads

2 tbsp water

5 oz/140 g ham, cut into strips

¾ cup heavy cream

½ cup freshly grated Parmesan cheese

2 egg yolks

salt and pepper

1 Bring a large, heavy-bottom pan of lightly salted water to a boil. Add the pasta, return to a boil, and cook for 8–10 minutes, or until tender but still firm to the bite.

2 Meanwhile, place the saffron in a separate heavy-bottom pan and add the water. Bring to a boil, then remove from the heat and let stand for 5 minutes.

3 Stir the ham, cream, and Parmesan cheese into the saffron and return the pan to the heat. Season to taste with salt and pepper and heat through gently, stirring continuously, until simmering. Remove the pan from the heat and beat in the egg yolks. Drain the pasta and transfer to a large, warmed serving dish. Add the saffron sauce, toss well, and serve immediately.

farfalle with gorgonzola & ham

SERVES 4

1 cup crème fraîche or sour cream

8 oz/225 g cremini mushrooms, quartered

14 oz/400 g dried farfalle

3 oz/85 g Gorgonzola cheese, crumbled

1 tbsp chopped fresh flat-leaf parsley, plus extra sprigs to garnish

6 oz/175 g cooked ham, diced

salt and pepper

1 Pour the crème fraîche into a pan, add the mushrooms, and season to taste with salt and pepper. Bring to just below a boil, then lower the heat and simmer very gently, stirring occasionally, for 8–10 minutes, until the cream has thickened.

2 Meanwhile, bring a large, heavy-bottom pan of lightly salted water to a boil. Add the pasta, return to a boil, and cook for 8–10 minutes, or until tender but still firm to the bite.

3 Remove the pan of mushrooms from the heat and stir in the Gorgonzola cheese until it has melted. Return the pan to very low heat and stir in the chopped parsley and ham.

4 Drain the pasta and add it to the sauce. Toss lightly, then divide among individual warmed dishes, garnish with the parsley sprigs, and serve immediately.

penne with ham, tomato & chile

SERVES 4

1 tbsp olive oil

2 tbsp butter

1 onion, finely chopped

5½ oz/150 g cooked
ham, diced

2 garlic cloves, very
finely chopped

1 red chile, seeded and
finely chopped

1 lb 12 oz/800 g of canned
chopped tomatoes

1 lb/450 g dried penne

2 tbsp chopped fresh
flat-leaf parsley

6 tbsp freshly grated
Parmesan cheese

salt and pepper

1 Put the olive oil and 1 tablespoon of the butter in a large skillet over medium–low heat. Add the onion and cook for 10 minutes, or until softened and golden. Add the ham and fry for an additional 5 minutes, or until lightly browned. Stir in the garlic, chile, and tomatoes. Season to taste with salt and pepper. Bring to a boil, then simmer over medium–low heat for 30–40 minutes, or until thickened.

2 Bring a large, heavy-bottom pan of lightly salted water to a boil. Add the pasta, return to a boil, and cook for 8–10 minutes, or until tender but still firm to the bite. Drain and transfer to a warmed serving dish.

3 Pour the sauce over the pasta. Add the parsley, Parmesan cheese, and the remaining butter. Toss well to mix and serve immediately.

sausage, bean & roasted squash conchiglie

SERVES 4

1 large butternut squash, peeled, seeded, and cut into chunks

3 tbsp olive oil

1 onion, finely chopped

1 celery stalk, finely chopped

8 oz/225 g pork sausages with herbs, skins removed

scant 1 cup red wine

generous 1 cup vegetable or chicken stock

3 tbsp sun-dried tomato paste

14 oz/400 g of canned borlotti beans, drained and rinsed

10 oz/280 g dried conchiglie (shells)

4 tbsp chopped fresh flat-leaf parsley

salt and pepper

freshly grated Romano cheese, to serve

1 Preheat the oven to 400°F/200°C. Put the squash in a roasting pan large enough to hold it in a single layer. Drizzle with 2 tablespoons of the olive oil. Toss together and roast for 25–30 minutes, or until tender.

2 Heat the remaining oil in a large skillet. Add the onion and celery and cook gently for 2 minutes, or until the onion turns translucent. Increase the heat and add the sausages. Cook for another 2–3 minutes, or until lightly browned, breaking the sausages into small pieces as you stir.

3 Add the wine to the skillet and boil rapidly until most of it has evaporated. Add the stock, tomato paste, and beans. Simmer for 10–12 minutes, or until the liquid has reduced and is slightly thickened.

4 Bring a large, heavy-bottom pan of lightly salted water to a boil. Add the pasta, return to a boil, and cook for 8–10 minutes, or until tender but still firm to the bite. Drain and transfer to a warmed serving bowl. Add the roasted squash, sausage sauce, and parsley, and season to taste. Serve immediately with the Romano cheese.

Step 1

Step 2

Step 3

rigatoni with chorizo & mushrooms

SERVES 4

4 tbsp olive oil

1 red onion, chopped

1 garlic clove, chopped

1 celery stalk, sliced

14 oz/400 g dried rigatoni (pasta tubes)

10 oz/280 g chorizo sausage, sliced

8 oz/225 g cremini mushrooms, halved

1 tbsp chopped fresh cilantro

1 tbsp lime juice

salt and pepper

1 Heat the oil in a skillet. Add the onion, garlic, and celery and cook over low heat, stirring occasionally, for 5 minutes, or until softened.

2 Meanwhile, bring a large, heavy-bottom pan of lightly salted water to a boil. Add the pasta, return to a boil, and cook for 8–10 minutes, or until tender but still firm to the bite.

3 While the pasta is cooking, add the chorizo to the skillet and cook, stirring occasionally, for 5 minutes, or until evenly browned. Add the mushrooms and cook, stirring occasionally, for an additional 5 minutes. Stir in the cilantro and lime juice and season to taste with salt and pepper.

4 Drain the pasta and return it to the pan. Add the chorizo and mushroom mixture and toss lightly. Divide among warmed serving dishes and serve immediately.

pepperoni pasta

SERVES 4

3 tbsp olive oil

1 onion, chopped

**1 red bell pepper, seeded
and diced**

**1 orange bell pepper,
seeded and diced**

**1 lb 12 oz/800 g of canned
chopped tomatoes**

**1 tbsp sun-dried tomato
paste**

1 tsp paprika

**8 oz/225 g pepperoni
sausage, sliced**

**2 tbsp chopped fresh
flat-leaf parsley, plus
extra to garnish**

1 lb/450 g dried penne

salt and pepper

1 Heat 2 tablespoons of the oil in a large, heavy-bottom skillet. Add the onion and cook over low heat, stirring occasionally, for 5 minutes, or until softened. Add the red and orange bell peppers, tomatoes and their can juices, sun-dried tomato paste, and paprika and bring to a boil.

2 Add the pepperoni and parsley and season to taste with salt and pepper. Stir well, bring to a boil, then reduce the heat and simmer for 10–15 minutes.

3 Meanwhile, bring a large, heavy-bottom pan of lightly salted water to a boil. Add the pasta, return to a boil, and cook for 8–10 minutes, or until tender but still firm to the bite. Drain well and transfer to a warmed serving dish. Add the remaining olive oil and toss. Add the sauce and toss again. Garnish with parsley and serve immediately.

penne with sausage sauce

SERVES 4–6

2 tbsp olive oil

1 red onion, coarsely chopped

2 garlic cloves, coarsely chopped

6 Italian sausages, skinned and the meat crumbled

½ tsp dried chile flakes

2 tbsp chopped fresh oregano

14 oz/400 g of canned chopped tomatoes

12 oz/350 g dried penne

salt and pepper

2 tbsp chopped fresh flat-leaf parsley, to garnish

3 tbsp freshly grated Parmesan cheese, to serve

1 Heat the oil in a large pan, then add the onion and cook over medium heat, stirring frequently, for 6–8 minutes, or until it starts to brown. Add the garlic and the crumbled sausages and cook for 8–10 minutes, breaking up the sausages with a wooden spoon.

2 Add the chile flakes and oregano and stir well. Pour in the tomatoes and bring to a boil, then reduce the heat and simmer, uncovered, for 4–5 minutes, or until reduced and thickened. Season to taste with salt and pepper.

3 Meanwhile, bring a large, heavy-bottom pan of lightly salted water to a boil. Add the pasta, return to a boil, and cook for 8–10 minutes, or until tender but still firm to the bite. Drain well and return the pasta to the pan.

4 Pour the sauce into the pasta and stir well. Transfer to warmed serving dishes, garnish with parsley, and serve immediately with Parmesan cheese.

linguine with lamb

SERVES 4

4 tomatoes

4 tbsp olive oil

10 oz/280 g boneless lamb, cubed

1 garlic clove, finely chopped

1 bay leaf

1 cup dry white wine

2 large yellow bell peppers, seeded and diced

9 oz/250 g dried linguine

salt and pepper

1 Chop the tomatoes into chunks. Heat half of the olive oil in a large, heavy-bottom skillet. Add the lamb and cook over medium heat, stirring frequently, until browned on all sides. Add the garlic and cook for an additional 1 minute. Add the bay leaf, pour in the wine, and season to taste with salt and pepper. Bring to a boil and cook for 5 minutes, or until reduced.

2 Stir in the remaining oil, bell peppers, and tomatoes. Reduce the heat, cover, and let simmer, stirring occasionally, for 45 minutes.

3 Meanwhile, bring a large, heavy-bottom pan of lightly salted water to a boil. Add the pasta, return to a boil, and cook for 8–10 minutes, or until tender but still firm to the bite. Drain and transfer to a warmed serving dish. Remove and discard the bay leaf from the lamb sauce and spoon the sauce on top of the pasta. Toss well and serve immediately.

Step 1

Step 1

Step 2

pasticcio

SERVES 4

1 tbsp olive oil

1 onion, chopped

2 garlic cloves, finely chopped

1 lb/450 g fresh ground lamb

2 tbsp tomato paste

2 tbsp all-purpose flour

1¼ cups chicken stock

1 tsp ground cinnamon

4 oz/115 g dried macaroni

2 beefsteak tomatoes, sliced

1¼ cups Greek yogurt

2 eggs, lightly beaten

salt and pepper

salad leaves, to serve

1 Preheat the oven to 375°F/190°C. Heat the oil in a large, heavy-bottom skillet. Add the onion and garlic and cook over low heat, stirring occasionally, for 5 minutes, or until softened. Add the lamb and cook, breaking it up with a wooden spoon, until browned all over. Add the tomato paste and sprinkle in the flour. Cook, stirring, for 1 minute, then stir in the stock. Season to taste with salt and pepper and stir in the cinnamon. Bring to a boil, reduce the heat, cover, and cook for 25 minutes.

2 Meanwhile, bring a large, heavy-bottom pan of lightly salted water to a boil. Add the pasta, return to a boil, and cook for 8–10 minutes, or until tender but still firm to the bite.

3 Drain the pasta and stir into the lamb mixture. Spoon into a large casserole dish and arrange the tomato slices on top. Beat together the yogurt and eggs, then spoon over the top of the lamb mixture. Bake in the preheated oven for 1 hour. Serve immediately with salad greens.

spaghetti with parsley chicken

SERVES 4

1 tbsp olive oil

thinly pared rind of 1 lemon, cut into julienne strips

1 tsp finely chopped fresh ginger

1 tsp sugar

1 cup chicken stock

9 oz/250 g dried spaghetti

4 tbsp butter

8 oz/225 g skinless, boneless chicken breasts, diced

1 red onion, finely chopped

leaves from 2 bunches of fresh flat-leaf parsley

salt

1 Heat the oil in a heavy-bottom pan. Add the lemon rind and cook over low heat, stirring frequently, for 5 minutes. Stir in the ginger and sugar, season to taste with salt, and cook, stirring continuously, for an additional 2 minutes. Pour in the chicken stock, bring to a boil, then cook for 5 minutes, or until the liquid has reduced by half.

2 Meanwhile, bring a large, heavy-bottom pan of lightly salted water to a boil. Add the pasta, return to a boil, and cook for 8–10 minutes, or until tender but still firm to the bite.

3 Melt half the butter in a skillet. Add the chicken and onion and cook, stirring frequently, for 5 minutes, or until the chicken is lightly browned all over. Stir in the lemon and ginger mixture and cook for 1 minute. Stir in the parsley leaves and cook, stirring continuously, for an additional 3 minutes.

4 Drain the pasta and transfer to a warmed serving dish, then add the remaining butter and toss well. Add the chicken sauce, toss again, and serve immediately.

farfalle with chicken, broccoli & peppers

SERVES 4

4 tbsp olive oil

5 tbsp butter

3 garlic cloves, very finely chopped

1 lb/450 g skinless, boneless chicken breasts, diced

¼ tsp dried chile flakes

1 bunch broccoli, cut into small florets

10½ oz/300 g dried farfalle

6 oz/175 g bottled roasted red bell peppers, drained and diced

1 cup chicken stock

salt and pepper

1 Bring a large, heavy-bottom pan of lightly salted water to a boil. Meanwhile, heat the oil and butter in a large skillet over medium–low heat. Add the garlic and cook until just beginning to color.

2 Add the diced chicken to the skillet, then raise the heat to medium and cook for 4–5 minutes, or until the chicken is no longer pink. Add the chile flakes and season to taste with salt and pepper. Remove from the heat.

3 Plunge the broccoli into the boiling water and cook for 2 minutes. Remove with a slotted spoon and set aside. Bring the water back to a boil. Add the pasta and cook for 8–10 minutes, or until tender but still firm to the bite. Drain and add to the chicken mixture in the pan. Add the broccoli and roasted bell peppers. Pour in the stock. Simmer briskly over medium–high heat, stirring frequently, until most of the liquid has been absorbed.

4 Transfer to warmed serving dishes and serve immediately.

pappardelle with chicken & porcini

SERVES 4

1½ oz/40 g dried porcini mushrooms

¾ cup hot water

1 lb 12 oz/800 g of canned chopped tomatoes

1 fresh red chile, seeded and finely chopped

3 tbsp olive oil

12 oz/350 g skinless, boneless chicken breasts, cut into thin strips

2 garlic cloves, finely chopped

12 oz/350 g dried pappardelle

salt and pepper

2 tbsp chopped fresh flat-leaf parsley, to garnish

1 Place the porcini in a small bowl, add the hot water, and let soak for 30 minutes. Meanwhile, place the tomatoes and their can juices in a heavy-bottom pan and break them up with a wooden spoon, then stir in the chile. Bring to a boil, then reduce the heat and let simmer, stirring occasionally, for 30 minutes, or until reduced.

2 Remove the mushrooms from their soaking liquid with a slotted spoon, reserving the liquid. Strain the liquid into the tomatoes, through a strainer lined with cheesecloth, and simmer for an additional 15 minutes. Meanwhile, heat 2 tablespoons of the olive oil in a heavy-bottom skillet. Add the chicken and cook, stirring frequently, until golden brown all over and tender. Stir in the mushrooms and garlic and cook for an additional 5 minutes.

3 Bring a large, heavy-bottom pan of lightly salted water to a boil. Add the pasta, return to a boil, and cook for 8–10 minutes, or until tender but still firm to the bite. Drain well, then transfer to a warmed serving dish. Drizzle with the remaining olive oil and toss lightly. Stir the chicken mixture into the tomato sauce, season, and spoon over the top of the pasta. Toss lightly, garnish with parsley, and serve immediately.

Step 1

Step 2

Step 2

italian chicken spirals

SERVES 4

**4 skinless, boneless
chicken breasts**

1 cup fresh basil leaves

1 tbsp hazelnuts

1 garlic clove, crushed

**9 oz/250 g dried
whole wheat fusilli**

**2 sun-dried tomatoes or
fresh tomatoes**

1 tbsp lemon juice

1 tbsp olive oil

1 tbsp capers

½ cup pitted black olives

salt and pepper

1 Beat the chicken breasts with a rolling pin to flatten evenly.

2 Place the basil and hazelnuts in a food processor and process until finely chopped. Mix with the garlic and salt and pepper to taste.

3 Spread the basil mixture over the chicken breasts and roll up from one short end to enclose the filling. Wrap each chicken roll tightly in foil so that they hold their shape, then seal the ends well.

4 Bring a large, heavy-bottom pan of lightly salted water to a boil. Add the pasta, return to a boil, and cook for 8–10 minutes, or until tender but still firm to the bite. Meanwhile, place the chicken parcels in a steamer or colander set over the pan, cover tightly, and steam for 10 minutes.

5 Using a sharp knife, dice the tomatoes. Drain the pasta and return to the pan with the lemon juice, oil, tomatoes, capers, and olives. Warm through. Pierce the chicken with a skewer to make sure that the juices run clear. Slice the chicken, arrange over top of the pasta in a warmed serving dish, and serve immediately.

chicken with creamy penne

SERVES 2

7 oz/200 g dried penne

1 tbsp olive oil

2 skinless, boneless chicken breasts

4 tbsp dry white wine

generous 1 cup frozen peas

5 tbsp heavy cream

salt

4–5 tbsp chopped fresh flat-leaf parsley, to garnish

1 Bring a large, heavy-bottom pan of lightly salted water to a boil. Add the pasta, return to a boil, and cook for 8–10 minutes, or until tender but still firm to the bite.

2 Meanwhile, heat the oil in a skillet, add the chicken breasts, and cook over medium heat for about 4 minutes on each side.

3 Pour in the wine and cook over high heat until it has almost evaporated.

4 Drain the pasta. Add the peas, cream, and pasta to the chicken breasts in the skillet and stir well. Cover and simmer for 2 minutes, or until the peas have cooked through. Serve immediately, garnished with chopped parsley.

fettuccine with chicken & onion cream sauce

SERVES 4

1 tbsp olive oil

2 tbsp butter

1 garlic clove, very finely chopped

4 skinless, boneless chicken breasts

1 onion, finely chopped

1 chicken bouillon cube, crumbled

½ cup water

1¼ cups heavy cream

¾ cup milk

6 scallions, green part included, sliced diagonally

⅓ cup freshly grated Parmesan cheese

1 lb/450 g dried fettuccine

salt and pepper

chopped fresh flat-leaf parsley, to garnish

1 Heat the oil and butter with the garlic in a large skillet over medium–low heat. Cook the garlic until just beginning to color. Add the chicken and raise the heat to medium. Cook for 4–5 minutes on each side, or until the juices are no longer pink. Season to taste with salt and pepper. Remove from the heat. Remove the chicken, leaving the oil in the skillet. Slice the chicken diagonally into thin strips and set aside.

2 Reheat the oil in the skillet. Add the onion and gently cook for 5 minutes, or until softened. Add the crumbled bouillon cube and the water. Bring to a boil, then simmer over medium–low heat for 10 minutes. Stir in the cream, milk, scallions, and Parmesan cheese. Simmer until heated through and slightly thickened.

3 Meanwhile, bring a large, heavy-bottom pan of lightly salted water to a boil. Add the pasta, return to a boil, and cook for 8–10 minutes, or until tender but still firm to the bite. Drain and transfer to a warmed serving dish. Layer the chicken slices over the pasta. Pour the sauce over the top, then garnish with parsley and serve immediately.

penne with chicken & feta

SERVES 4

2 tbsp olive oil

1 lb/450 g skinless, boneless chicken breasts, cut into thin strips

6 scallions, chopped

8 oz/225 g feta cheese, diced

4 tbsp snipped fresh chives

1 lb/450 g dried penne

salt and pepper

1 Heat the oil in a heavy-bottom skillet. Add the chicken and cook over medium heat, stirring frequently, for 5–8 minutes, or until golden all over and cooked through. Add the scallions and cook for 2 minutes. Stir the feta cheese into the skillet with half of the chives and season to taste with salt and pepper.

2 Meanwhile, bring a large, heavy-bottom pan of lightly salted water to a boil. Add the pasta, return to a boil, and cook for 8–10 minutes, or until tender but still firm to the bite. Drain well, then transfer to a warmed serving dish.

3 Spoon the chicken mixture onto the pasta, toss lightly, and serve immediately, garnished with the remaining chives.

VARIATION
Replace the chicken with the same weight of turkey, cut into thin strips. The feta can then be replaced with ricotta cheese, crumbled into the pan.

3

Fabulous
Fish &
Seafood

conchiglie with smoked salmon & sour cream

SERVES 4

**1 lb/450 g dried
conchiglie (shells)**

1¼ cups sour cream

2 tsp whole grain mustard

**4 large scallions,
finely sliced**

**8 oz/225 g smoked salmon,
cut into bite-size pieces**

**finely grated rind of
½ lemon**

salt and pepper

**2 tbsp snipped fresh
chives, to garnish**

1 Bring a large, heavy-bottom pan of lightly salted water to a boil. Add the pasta, return to a boil, and cook for 8–10 minutes, or until tender but still firm to the bite. Drain and return to the pan.

2 Add the sour cream, mustard, scallions, smoked salmon, and lemon rind to the pasta. Stir over low heat until heated through. Season to taste with pepper.

3 Transfer to a warmed serving dish and garnish with the chives. Serve warm or at room temperature.

tagliatelle with smoked salmon & arugula

SERVES 4

**12 oz/350 g dried
tagliatelle**

2 tbsp olive oil

**1 garlic clove, finely
chopped**

**4 oz/115 g smoked salmon,
cut into thin strips**

1¼ cups arugula

salt and pepper

1 Bring a large, heavy-bottom pan of lightly salted water to a boil. Add the pasta, return to a boil, and cook for 8–10 minutes, or until tender but still firm to the bite.

2 Just before the end of the cooking time, heat the olive oil in a heavy-bottom skillet. Add the garlic and cook over low heat, stirring continuously, for 1 minute. Do not let the garlic brown or it will taste bitter.

3 Add the salmon and arugula. Season to taste with pepper and cook, stirring continuously, for 1 minute. Remove the skillet from the heat.

4 Drain the pasta and transfer to a large, warmed serving dish. Add the smoked salmon and arugula mixture, toss lightly, and serve immediately.

sea bass with olive sauce

SERVES 4

1 lb/450 g dried macaroni

1 tbsp olive oil

8 x 4 oz/115 g sea bass medallions

shredded leek and shredded carrot, to garnish

salt

sauce

2 tbsp butter

4 shallots, chopped

2 tbsp capers

1½ cups chopped, pitted green olives

4 tbsp balsamic vinegar

1¼ cups fish stock

1¼ cups heavy cream

juice of 1 lemon

salt and pepper

1 To make the sauce, melt the butter in a skillet. Add the shallots and cook over low heat for 4 minutes. Add the capers and olives and cook for an additional 3 minutes.

2 Stir in the balsamic vinegar and fish stock. Bring to a boil and reduce by half. Add the cream, stirring continuously, and reduce again by half. Season to taste with salt and pepper and stir in the lemon juice. Remove the skillet from the heat; set aside and keep warm.

3 Bring a large, heavy-bottom pan of lightly salted water to a boil. Add the pasta and olive oil, return to a boil, and cook for 8–10 minutes, or until tender but still firm to the bite.

4 Meanwhile, preheat the broiler to high, then lightly broil the sea bass medallions for 3–4 minutes on each side, or until cooked through, but still moist and delicate.

5 Drain the pasta thoroughly and transfer to warmed serving dishes. Top the pasta with the fish medallions and pour the olive sauce over the top. Garnish with shredded leek and carrot and serve immediately.

fettuccine with sole & monkfish

SERVES 4

generous ½ cup all-purpose flour

1 lb/450 g lemon sole fillets, skinned and cut into chunks

1 lb/450 g monkfish fillets, skinned and cut into chunks

6 tbsp unsalted butter

4 shallots, finely chopped

2 garlic cloves, crushed

1 carrot, diced

1 leek, finely chopped

1¼ cups fish stock

1¼ cups dry white wine

2 tsp anchovy extract

1 tbsp balsamic vinegar

1 lb/450 g dried fettuccine

chopped fresh flat-leaf parsley, to garnish

salt and pepper

1 Season the flour with salt and pepper and spread out 2 tablespoons of the mixture on a plate. Coat all the fish pieces with it, shaking off the excess. Melt the butter in a heavy-bottom skillet or flameproof casserole. Add the fish, shallots, garlic, carrot, and leek, then cook over low heat, stirring frequently, for 10 minutes. Sprinkle in the remaining seasoned flour and cook, stirring continuously, for 1 minute.

2 Mix the fish stock, wine, anchovy extract, and balsamic vinegar together in a pitcher and gradually stir into the fish mixture. Bring to a boil, stirring continuously, then reduce the heat and let simmer gently for 35 minutes.

3 Meanwhile, bring a large, heavy-bottom pan of lightly salted water to a boil. Add the pasta, return to a boil, and cook for 8–10 minutes, or until tender but still firm to the bite. Drain and transfer to a warmed serving dish. Spoon the fish mixture onto the pasta, garnish with chopped parsley, and serve immediately.

Step
1

Step
1

Step
2

fusilli with monkfish & broccoli

SERVES 4

1½ cups broccoli florets

3 tbsp olive oil

12 oz/350 g monkfish fillet, skinned and cut into bite-size pieces

2 garlic cloves, crushed

½ cup dry white wine

1 cup heavy cream

14 oz/400 g dried fusilli

3 oz/85 g Gorgonzola cheese, diced

salt and pepper

1 Bring a pan of lightly salted water to a boil, add the broccoli, and cook for 2 minutes. Drain and refresh under cold running water.

2 Heat the oil in a large, heavy-bottom skillet. Add the monkfish and garlic and season to taste with salt and pepper. Cook, stirring frequently, for 5 minutes, or until the fish is opaque. Pour in the white wine and cream and cook, stirring occasionally, for 5 minutes, or until the fish is cooked through and the sauce has thickened. Stir in the broccoli.

3 Meanwhile, bring a large, heavy-bottom pan of lightly salted water to a boil. Add the pasta, return to a boil, and cook for 8–10 minutes, or until tender but still firm to the bite. Drain and turn the pasta into the pan with the fish, add the cheese, and toss lightly. Serve immediately.

baked tuna & ricotta rigatoni

SERVES 4

butter, for greasing

**1 lb/450 g dried rigatoni
(pasta tubes)**

**7 oz/200 g of canned tuna,
drained and flaked**

1 cup ricotta cheese

½ cup heavy cream

**2 cups freshly grated
Parmesan cheese**

**¾ cup drained and sliced
sun-dried tomatoes in oil**

salt and pepper

1 Preheat the oven to 400°F/200°C. Lightly grease a large, ovenproof dish with butter. Bring a large, heavy-bottom pan of lightly salted water to a boil. Add the rigatoni, return to a boil, and cook for 8–10 minutes, or until tender but still firm to the bite. Drain the pasta and let stand until cool enough to handle.

2 Meanwhile, mix the tuna and ricotta cheese together in a bowl to form a soft paste. Spoon the mixture into a pastry bag and use to fill the rigatoni. Arrange the filled pasta tubes side by side in the prepared dish.

3 To make the sauce, mix the cream and Parmesan cheese together in a bowl and season to taste with salt and pepper. Spoon the sauce over the top of the rigatoni and top with the sun-dried tomatoes, arranged in a crisscross pattern. Bake in the preheated oven for 20 minutes. Serve immediately, straight from the dish.

spaghetti with tuna & parsley

SERVES 6

1 lb 2 oz/500 g dried spaghetti

2 tbsp butter

7 oz/200 g of canned tuna, drained

2 oz/55 g of canned anchovy fillets, drained

1 cup olive oil

1 cup coarsely chopped fresh flat-leaf parsley, plus extra to garnish

⅔ cup sour cream or yogurt

salt and pepper

1 Bring a large, heavy-bottom pan of lightly salted water to a boil. Add the spaghetti, return to a boil, and cook for 8–10 minutes, or until tender but still firm to the bite. Drain the spaghetti and return to the pan. Add the butter, toss thoroughly to coat, and keep warm until needed.

2 Flake the tuna into smaller pieces using two forks. Place the tuna in a food processor or blender with the anchovies, oil, and parsley and process until the sauce is smooth. Pour in the sour cream and process for a few seconds to blend. Taste the sauce and season with salt and pepper, if necessary.

3 Shake the pan of spaghetti over medium heat for a few minutes, or until it is thoroughly warmed through.

4 Pour the sauce over the top of the spaghetti and toss quickly, using two forks. Garnish with parsley and serve immediately.

pasta with tuna & olives

SERVES 4

12 oz/350 g dried conchiglie (shells) or gnocchi

4 tbsp olive oil

4 tbsp butter

3 large garlic cloves, thinly sliced

7 oz/200 g of canned tuna, drained and broken into chunks

2 tbsp lemon juice

1 tbsp capers, drained

10–12 black olives, pitted and chopped

2 tbsp chopped fresh flat-leaf parsley

salt

1 Bring a large, heavy-bottom saucepan of lightly salted water to a boil. Add the pasta, return to a boil, and cook for 8–10 minutes, or until tender but still firm to the bite. Drain and return to the pan. Heat the olive oil and half of the butter in a skillet over medium–low heat. Add the garlic and cook for a few seconds.

2 Reduce the heat to low. Flake the tuna into smaller pieces using two forks. Add the tuna, lemon juice, capers, and olives to the skillet.

3 Stir the tuna mixture continuously until it is heated through. Transfer the pasta or gnocchi to a warmed serving dish. Pour the tuna mixture over the pasta. Add the parsley and remaining butter. Toss well to mix. Serve immediately.

Step 2

Step 2

Step 3

spaghettini with quick tuna sauce

SERVES 4

3 tbsp olive oil

4 tomatoes, peeled, seeded, and coarsely chopped

1⅔ cups sliced white mushrooms

1 tbsp chopped fresh basil

14 oz/400 g of canned tuna, drained and flaked

⅓ cup fish or chicken stock

1 garlic clove, finely chopped

2 tsp chopped fresh marjoram

12 oz/350 g dried spaghettini

salt and pepper

1 cup freshly grated Parmesan cheese, to serve

1 Heat the oil in a large skillet. Add the tomatoes and cook over low heat, stirring occasionally, for 15 minutes, or until pulpy. Add the mushrooms and cook, stirring occasionally, for an additional 10 minutes. Stir in the basil, tuna, stock, garlic, and marjoram, and season to taste with salt and pepper. Cook over low heat for 5 minutes, or until heated through.

2 Meanwhile, bring a large, heavy-bottom pan of lightly salted water to a boil. Add the pasta, return to a boil, and cook for 8–10 minutes, or until tender but still firm to the bite.

3 Drain the pasta well, transfer to a warmed serving dish, and spoon the tuna mixture over the top. Serve immediately with grated Parmesan cheese.

penne with sicilian sauce

SERVES 4

½ **cup raisins**

4 tomatoes, halved

¼ **cup pine nuts**

1¾ **oz/50 g of canned
anchovy fillets, drained
and halved lengthwise**

2 tbsp tomato paste

12 oz/350 g dried penne

salt

1 Soak the raisins in a bowl of warm water for about 20 minutes. Drain them thoroughly.

2 Preheat the broiler, then cook the tomatoes under the hot broiler for 10 minutes. Let cool slightly, then once cool enough to handle, peel off the skin and dice the flesh. Place the pine nuts on a cookie sheet and lightly toast under the broiler for 2–3 minutes, or until golden brown.

3 Place the tomatoes, pine nuts, and raisins in a small pan and heat gently. Add the anchovies and tomato paste, and cook the sauce over low heat for an additional 2–3 minutes, or until hot.

4 Meanwhile, bring a large, heavy-bottom pan of lightly salted water to a boil. Add the pasta, return to a boil, and cook for 8–10 minutes, or until tender but still firm to the bite. Drain thoroughly, then transfer the pasta to a warmed serving dish and serve immediately with the Sicilian tomato sauce.

fettuccine with spinach & anchovies

SERVES 4

2 lb/900 g fresh baby spinach leaves

14 oz/400 g dried fettuccine

5 tbsp olive oil

3 tbsp pine nuts

3 garlic cloves, crushed

8 canned anchovy fillets, drained and chopped

salt

1 Trim off any tough spinach stems. Rinse the spinach leaves under cold running water and place them in a large pan with only the water that is clinging to them after washing. Cover and cook over high heat, shaking the pan from time to time, until the spinach has wilted, but retains its color. Drain well, set aside, and keep warm.

2 Bring a large, heavy-bottom pan of lightly salted water to a boil. Add the fettuccine, return to a boil, and cook for 8–10 minutes, or until tender but still firm to the bite.

3 Heat 4 tablespoons of the oil in a separate pan. Add the pine nuts and cook until golden. Remove the pine nuts from the pan and set aside until needed.

4 Add the garlic to the pan and cook until golden. Add the anchovies and stir in the spinach. Cook, stirring continuously, for 2–3 minutes, or until heated through. Return the pine nuts to the pan.

5 Drain the fettuccine, toss in the remaining oil, and transfer to a warmed serving dish. Spoon the anchovy and spinach sauce over the fettuccine, toss lightly, and serve immediately.

farfalle with salmon & vegetables

SERVES 2

7 oz/200 g asparagus, trimmed

1 tbsp lemon juice

1 tbsp olive oil

1 large zucchini, thinly sliced diagonally

5½ oz/150 g dried farfalle

scant ½ cup crème fraîche or sour cream

thinly pared rind of 1 lemon

⅔ cup baby spinach leaves

7 oz/200 g salmon fillets, skinned and cut into bite-size pieces

salt and pepper

1 Preheat a grill pan until smoking hot. If the asparagus spears are plump, carefully slice them in half lengthwise.

2 Combine the lemon juice and olive oil in a bowl. Add the asparagus and zucchini, season to taste with salt and pepper, and toss together. Cook the vegetables in batches on the grill pan for 2–3 minutes on each side, or until tender. Transfer to a warmed plate and keep hot.

3 Bring a large, heavy-bottom pan of lightly salted water to a boil. Add the pasta, return to a boil, and cook for 8–10 minutes, or until tender but still firm to the bite. Drain and set aside. Heat the crème fraîche and lemon rind in the same pan until melted. Add the baby spinach leaves to the pan, followed by the pasta, charbroiled vegetables, and salmon. Season to taste with salt and pepper and toss well. Serve immediately.

Step 2

Step 2

Step 3

spaghetti alla puttanesca

SERVES 4

3 tbsp olive oil

**2 garlic cloves, finely
chopped**

**10 canned anchovy fillets,
drained and chopped**

**1 cup black olives, pitted
and chopped**

**1 tbsp capers, drained and
rinsed**

**8 plum tomatoes, peeled,
seeded, and chopped**

14 oz/400 g dried spaghetti

cayenne pepper and salt

**2 tbsp chopped fresh
flat-leaf parsley,
to garnish (optional)**

1 Heat the oil in a heavy-bottom skillet. Add the garlic and cook over low heat, stirring frequently, for 2 minutes. Add the anchovies and mash them to a pulp with a fork. Add the olives, capers, and tomatoes, and season to taste with cayenne pepper. Cover and simmer for 25 minutes.

2 Meanwhile, bring a large, heavy-bottom pan of lightly salted water to a boil. Add the pasta, return to a boil, and cook for 8–10 minutes, or until tender but still firm to the bite. Drain well and transfer to a warmed serving dish.

3 Spoon the anchovy sauce into the dish and toss with the pasta, using two large forks. Garnish with the chopped parsley, if using, and serve immediately.

macaroni with scallops & pine nuts

SERVES 4

14 oz/400 g dried long macaroni

4 tbsp olive oil

1 garlic clove, finely chopped

¼ cup pine nuts

8 large prepared scallops, sliced

salt and pepper

2 tbsp shredded fresh basil leaves, to garnish

1 Bring a large, heavy-bottom saucepan of lightly salted water to a boil. Add the pasta, return to a boil, and cook for 8–10 minutes, or until tender but still firm to the bite.

2 About 5 minutes before the pasta is ready, heat the oil in a skillet. Add the garlic and cook for 1–2 minutes, or until softened but not browned. Add the pine nuts and cook until browned. Stir in the scallops and cook until just opaque. Season to taste with salt and pepper.

3 When the pasta is cooked, drain and return to the saucepan. Add the contents of the skillet to the pasta and toss together. Serve garnished with the shredded basil leaves.

pappardelle with scallops & porcini

SERVES 4

**1⅓ cups dried porcini
mushrooms**

2 cups hot water

3 tbsp olive oil

3 tbsp butter

**1½ cups prepared scallops,
sliced**

**2 garlic cloves,
very finely chopped**

2 tbsp lemon juice

1 cup heavy cream

**12 oz/350 g dried
pappardelle**

salt and pepper

**2 tbsp chopped fresh
flat-leaf parsley,
to garnish**

1 Put the porcini mushrooms and hot water in a bowl. Let soak for 20 minutes. Strain the mushrooms, reserving the soaking water, and chop coarsely. Strain the liquid through a cheesecloth-lined, fine-mesh strainer into a bowl.

2 Heat the oil and butter in a large skillet over medium heat. Add the scallops and cook for 2 minutes, or until just golden. Add the garlic and mushrooms, then cook for another minute.

3 Stir in the lemon juice, cream, and ½ cup of the strained mushroom water. Bring to a boil, then simmer over medium heat for 2–3 minutes, stirring continuously, or until the liquid is reduced by half. Season to taste with salt and pepper. Remove from the heat.

4 Meanwhile, bring a large, heavy-bottom pan of lightly salted water to a boil. Add the pasta, return to a boil, and cook for 8–10 minutes, or until tender but still firm to the bite. Drain and transfer to a warmed serving dish. Briefly reheat the sauce and pour over the top of the pasta. Garnish with the parsley and toss well to mix. Serve immediately.

spaghetti with shrimp & garlic

SERVES 4

3 tbsp olive oil

3 tbsp butter

4 garlic cloves, finely chopped

2 tbsp seeded and finely chopped red bell pepper

2 tbsp tomato paste

½ cup dry white wine

1 lb/450 g spaghetti

12 oz/350 g raw shrimp, peeled and deveined

½ cup heavy cream

salt and pepper

3 tbsp chopped fresh flat-leaf parsley, to garnish

1 Heat the oil and butter in a skillet over medium–low heat. Add the garlic and red bell pepper. Fry for a few seconds until the garlic is just beginning to color. Stir in the tomato paste and wine. Cook for 10 minutes, stirring occasionally.

2 Bring a large, heavy-bottom pan of lightly salted water to a boil. Add the pasta, return to a boil, and cook for 8–10 minutes, or until tender but still firm to the bite. Drain and return to the pan.

3 Add the shrimp to the sauce and raise the heat to medium–high. Cook for 2 minutes, stirring continuously, until the shrimp turn pink. Reduce the heat and stir in the cream. Cook for 1 minute, stirring continuously, until thickened. Season to taste with salt and pepper.

4 Transfer the spaghetti to a warmed serving dish and pour the sauce over the top. Garnish with the parsley. Toss well to mix and serve immediately.

Step 1

Step 2

Step 3

linguine with shrimp & scallops

SERVES 6

1 lb/450 g raw shrimp

2 tbsp butter

2 shallots, finely chopped

1 cup dry white vermouth

1½ cups water

1 lb/450 g dried linguine

2 tbsp olive oil

1 lb/450 g prepared scallops

2 tbsp snipped fresh chives, plus chive flowers, to garnish

salt and pepper

1 Peel and devein the shrimp, reserving the shells. Melt the butter in a heavy-bottom skillet. Add the shallots and cook over low heat, stirring occasionally, for 5 minutes, or until softened. Add the shrimp shells and cook, stirring continuously, for 1 minute. Pour in the vermouth and cook, stirring continuously, for 1 minute. Add the water, bring to a boil, then reduce the heat and let simmer for 10 minutes, or until the liquid has reduced by half. Remove the skillet from the heat.

2 Bring a large, heavy-bottom pan of lightly salted water to a boil. Add the pasta, return to a boil, and cook for 8–10 minutes, or until tender but still firm to the bite.

3 Meanwhile, heat the oil in a separate heavy-bottom skillet. Add the scallops and shrimp and cook, stirring frequently, for 2 minutes, or until the scallops are opaque and the shrimp turn pink. Strain the shrimp-shell stock into the skillet. Drain the pasta and add to the skillet with the chives, then season to taste with salt and pepper. Toss well over low heat for 1 minute, then serve immediately, garnished with a chive flower.

fusilli with shrimp & peas

SERVES 4

pinch of saffron threads

1 cup dry white wine

3 tbsp olive oil

2 tbsp unsalted butter

1 shallot, chopped

2 cups peas

12 oz/350 g cooked shrimp

12 oz/350 g dried fusilli

salt and pepper

2 tbsp chopped fresh dill, to garnish

1 Place the saffron in a small bowl, add the wine, and let soak. Heat the olive oil and butter in a large, heavy-bottom skillet. Add the shallot and cook over low heat, stirring occasionally, for 5 minutes, or until softened. Add the peas and shrimp and cook, stirring occasionally, for 2–3 minutes.

2 Bring a large, heavy-bottom pan of lightly salted water to a boil. Add the pasta, return to a boil, and cook for 8–10 minutes, or until tender but still firm to the bite.

3 Meanwhile, stir the saffron and wine mixture into the skillet. Increase the heat and cook until the liquid is reduced by about half. Season to taste with salt and pepper. Drain the pasta and add to the skillet. Cook for 1–2 minutes, or until it is well coated with the sauce. Transfer to a warmed serving dish, sprinkle with dill, and serve immediately.

tagliatelle with creamy shrimp

SERVES 4

3 tbsp olive oil

3 tbsp butter

4 garlic cloves, very finely chopped

2 tbsp seeded and finely chopped red bell pepper

2 tbsp tomato paste

½ cup dry white wine

1 lb/450 g dried tagliatelle

12 oz/350 g raw shrimp, peeled and deveined, cut into ½-inch/1-cm pieces

½ cup heavy cream

salt and pepper

3 tbsp chopped fresh flat-leaf parsley, to garnish

1 Heat the oil and butter in a pan over medium–low heat. Add the garlic and red bell pepper. Cook for a few seconds, or until the garlic is just beginning to color. Stir in the tomato paste and wine. Cook for 10 minutes, stirring continuously.

2 Meawhile, bring a large, heavy-bottom pan of lightly salted water to a boil. Add the pasta, return to a boil, and cook for 8–10 minutes, or until tender but still firm to the bite. Drain and return to the pan.

3 Add the shrimp to the sauce and raise the heat to medium–high. Cook for 2 minutes, stirring continuously, or until the shrimp turn pink. Reduce the heat and stir in the cream. Cook for 1 minute, stirring continuously, or until thickened. Season to taste with salt and pepper.

4 Transfer the pasta to a warmed serving dish. Pour the sauce over the top of the pasta. Garnish with the parsley. Toss well to mix and serve immediately.

tagliatelle with mussels in white wine

SERVES 4

**4 lb 8 oz/2 kg mussels,
scrubbed and debearded**

1 large onion, chopped

**3 garlic cloves, finely
chopped**

2¼ cups dry white wine

1 bay leaf

2 sprigs of fresh thyme

**5 tbsp chopped fresh
flat-leaf parsley**

**1 tbsp chopped fresh
rosemary**

4 tbsp butter

1 lb/450 g dried tagliatelle

salt and pepper

1 Rinse the mussels well, discarding any with broken shells or that remain open when tapped.

2 Put the onion, garlic, white wine, herbs, and 2 tablespoons of the butter in a pan. Bring to a boil, then reduce the heat. Add the mussels, then season to taste with salt and pepper. Cover and cook over medium heat for 3–4 minutes, shaking the pan, or until the mussels open. Remove from the heat. Lift out the mussels with a slotted spoon, reserving the liquid. Discard any that remain closed. Remove most of the others from their shells, reserving a few in their shells to garnish.

3 Bring a large, heavy-bottom pan of lightly salted water to a boil. Add the pasta, return to a boil, and cook for 8–10 minutes, or until tender but still firm to the bite. Divide the pasta between four warmed serving bowls. Spoon the mussels over the top of the pasta. Strain the mussel liquid and return to the pan. Add the remaining butter and heat until melted. Pour over the top of the pasta, garnish with the mussels in their shells, and serve immediately.

Step 1

Step 2

Step 2

penne with squid & tomatoes

SERVES 4

8 oz/225 g dried penne

12 oz/350 g prepared squid

6 tbsp olive oil

2 onions, sliced

**1 cup fish stock or
chicken stock**

⅔ cup red wine

**14 oz/400 g of canned
chopped tomatoes**

2 tbsp tomato paste

**1 tbsp chopped fresh
marjoram**

1 bay leaf

salt and pepper

**2 tbsp chopped fresh
flat-leaf parsley,
to garnish**

1 Bring a large, heavy-bottom pan of lightly salted water to a boil. Add the pasta, return to a boil, and cook for 3 minutes, then drain and set aside until ready to use. With a sharp knife, cut the squid into strips.

2 Heat the olive oil in a large saucepan. Add the onions and cook over low heat, stirring occasionally, for 5 minutes, or until softened. Add the squid and stock, bring to a boil, and simmer for 3 minutes. Stir in the wine, chopped tomatoes and their can juices, tomato paste, marjoram, and bay leaf. Season to taste with salt and pepper. Bring to a boil and cook for 5 minutes, or until slightly reduced.

3 Add the pasta, return to a boil, and simmer for 8–10 minutes, or until tender but still firm to the bite. Remove and discard the bay leaf. Transfer to a warmed serving dish, garnish with the parsley, and serve immediately.

spaghetti with crab

SERVES 4

**1 dressed crab, about 1 lb/
450 g, including the shell**

12 oz/350 g dried spaghetti

6 tbsp extra virgin olive oil

**1 red chile, seeded and
finely chopped**

**2 garlic cloves, finely
chopped**

**3 tbsp chopped fresh
flat-leaf parsley**

2 tbsp lemon juice

**1 tsp finely grated lemon
rind**

salt and pepper

lemon wedges, to garnish

1 Using a knife, scoop the meat from the crab shell into a bowl. Mix the white and brown meat lightly together and set aside.

2 Bring a large, heavy-bottom pan of lightly salted water to a boil. Add the pasta, return to a boil, and cook for 8–10 minutes, or until tender but still firm to the bite. Drain thoroughly and return to the pan.

3 Meanwhile, heat 2 tablespoons of the oil in a skillet over low heat. Add the chile and garlic and cook for 30 seconds, then add the crabmeat, parsley, lemon juice, and lemon rind. Cook for an additional minute, or until the crabmeat is just heated through.

4 Add the crab mixture to the pasta with the remaining oil and season to taste with salt and pepper. Toss together thoroughly, then transfer to a warmed serving dish. Garnish with a few lemon wedges and serve immediately.

linguine with mixed seafood

SERVES 4–6

2 tbsp olive oil

2 shallots, finely chopped

2 garlic cloves, finely chopped

1 small red chile, seeded and finely chopped

7 oz/200 g of canned chopped tomatoes

3 tbsp chopped fresh flat-leaf parsley, plus extra sprigs to garnish

pinch of sugar

1 lb/450 g live mussels, scrubbed and debearded

6 tbsp dry white wine

1 lemon, sliced

1 lb/450 g clams, scrubbed

1 lb/450 g dried linguine

6 oz/175 g large cooked, peeled shrimp

salt and pepper

1 Heat the olive oil in a saucepan. Add the shallots, garlic, and chile and cook over low heat, stirring occasionally, for 5 minutes. Increase the heat to medium, stir in the tomatoes, chopped parsley, and sugar and season to taste with salt and pepper. Bring to a boil, then cover and simmer, stirring occasionally, for 15–20 minutes.

2 Discard any mussels with broken shells or any that refuse to close when tapped. Pour the wine into a large saucepan with a tight-fitting lid and add the lemon slices, mussels, and clams. Cover and cook over high heat, shaking the pan occasionally, for 5 minutes, or until all the shellfish have opened. Using a slotted spoon, transfer the shellfish to a bowl and reserve the cooking liquid.

3 Discard any mussels and clams that remain closed. Reserve a few for the garnish and remove the remainder from their shells. Strain the cooking liquid through a cheesecloth-lined, fine-mesh strainer. Bring a large, heavy-bottom pan of lightly salted water to a boil. Add the pasta, return to a boil, and cook for 8–10 minutes, or until tender but still firm to the bite.

4 Meanwhile, stir the strained cooking liquid into the tomato mixture and bring to a boil, stirring continuously. Add the shelled mussel and clams, and the shrimp. Season and heat through. Drain the pasta and return it to the pan. Add the shellfish mixture and toss well. Garnish with the reserved mussels and clams and parsley. Serve immediately.

spaghetti con vongole

SERVES 4

2 lb 4 oz/1 kg clams, scrubbed

¾ cup water

¾ cup dry white wine

12 oz/350 g dried spaghetti

5 tbsp olive oil

2 garlic cloves, finely chopped

4 tbsp chopped fresh flat-leaf parsley

salt and pepper

1 Discard any clams with broken shells or any that refuse to close when tapped. Place the clams in a large, heavy-bottom pan. Add the water and wine, then cover and cook over high heat, shaking the pan occasionally, for 5 minutes, or until the shells have opened. Remove the clams with a slotted spoon and strain the liquid through a cheesecloth-lined, fine-mesh strainer into a small pan. Bring to a boil and cook until reduced by about half. Discard any clams that remain closed and remove the remainder from their shells.

2 Bring a large, heavy-bottom pan of lightly salted water to a boil. Add the pasta, return to a boil, and cook for 8–10 minutes, or until tender but still firm to the bite.

3 Meanwhile, heat the oil in a large, heavy-bottom skillet. Add the garlic and cook, stirring frequently, for 2 minutes. Add the parsley and the reduced clam cooking liquid and simmer gently. Drain the pasta and add it to the skillet with the clams. Season to taste with salt and pepper and cook, stirring continuously, for 4 minutes, or until the pasta is coated and the clams have heated through. Transfer to a warmed serving dish and serve immediately.

VARIATION

Replace the clams with scrubbed and debearded mussels. Discard any that do not close when tapped. After cooking, discard any that stay closed.

4

Vibrant Vegetarian

tagliatelle with pesto

SERVES 4

1 lb/450 g dried tagliatelle

salt

**fresh basil sprigs,
to garnish**

pesto

2 garlic cloves

¼ cup pine nuts

1½ cups fresh basil leaves

½ cup olive oil

**½ cup freshly grated
Parmesan-style
vegetarian cheese**

salt

1 To make the pesto, put the garlic, pine nuts, and a large pinch of salt into a food processor or blender and process briefly. Add the basil leaves and process to a paste. With the motor still running, gradually add the oil. Scrape into a bowl and beat in the cheese. Season to taste with salt.

2 Bring a large, heavy-bottom pan of lightly salted water to a boil. Add the pasta, return to a boil, and cook for 8–10 minutes, or until tender but still firm to the bite. Drain the pasta well, return to the pan, and toss with half of the pesto, then divide among warmed serving dishes and top with the remaining pesto. Garnish with basil and serve immediately.

fusilli with sun-dried tomatoes

SERVES 4

3 oz/85 g sun-dried tomatoes (not in oil)

3 cups boiling water

2 tbsp olive oil

1 onion, finely chopped

2 large garlic cloves, finely sliced

2 tbsp chopped fresh flat-leaf parsley

2 tsp chopped fresh oregano

1 tsp chopped fresh rosemary

12 oz/350 g dried fusilli

10 fresh basil leaves, shredded

salt and pepper

3 tbsp freshly grated Parmesan-style vegetarian cheese, to serve

1 Put the sun-dried tomatoes in a bowl, pour the boiling water over the top, and let stand for 5 minutes. Using a slotted spoon, remove one third of the tomatoes from the bowl. Cut into bite-size pieces. Put the remaining tomatoes and water into a food processor or blender and process until the mixture is a puree.

2 Heat the oil in a large skillet over medium heat. Add the onion and cook gently for 5 minutes, or until softened. Add the garlic and cook until just beginning to color. Add the pureed tomato and the reserved tomato pieces to the skillet. Bring to a boil, then simmer over medium–low heat for 10 minutes. Stir in the herbs and season to taste with salt and pepper. Simmer for 1 minute, then remove from the heat.

3 Bring a large, heavy-bottom pan of lightly salted water to a boil. Add the pasta, return to a boil, and cook for 8–10 minutes, or until tender but still firm to the bite. Drain and transfer to a warmed serving dish. Briefly reheat the sauce. Pour over the top of the pasta, then add the basil and toss well to mix. Sprinkle with the cheese and serve immediately.

spaghetti olio e aglio

SERVES 4

1 lb/450 g dried spaghetti

½ cup extra virgin olive oil

3 garlic cloves, finely chopped

3 tbsp chopped fresh flat-leaf parsley

salt and pepper

1 Bring a large, heavy-bottom pan of lightly salted water to a boil. Add the pasta, return to a boil, and cook for 8–10 minutes, or until tender but still firm to the bite.

2 Meanwhile, heat the oil in a heavy-bottom skillet. Add the garlic and a pinch of salt and cook over low heat, stirring continuously, for 3–4 minutes, or until golden. Do not let the garlic brown or it will taste bitter. Remove the skillet from the heat.

3 Drain the pasta and transfer to a warmed serving dish. Pour in the garlic-flavored olive oil, then add the chopped parsley and season to taste with salt and pepper. Toss well and serve immediately.

pasta with leek & butternut squash

SERVES 4

1¾ cups sliced baby leeks, about ¾-inch/2-cm thick

1¾ cups butternut squash chunks, about ¾-inch/ 2-cm square

1½ tbsp medium curry paste

1 tsp vegetable oil

10 cherry tomatoes

9 oz/250 g dried farfalle

2 tbsp chopped fresh cilantro leaves

salt

white sauce

generous 1 cup skim milk

2 tbsp cornstarch

1 tsp mustard powder

1 small onion, left whole

2 small bay leaves

4 tsp grated Parmesan-style vegetarian cheese

1 To make the white sauce, put the milk into a small pan with the cornstarch, mustard powder, onion, and bay leaves. Whisk over medium heat until thick. Remove from the heat, discard the onion and bay leaves, and stir in the cheese. Set aside, stirring occasionally to prevent a skin forming. Preheat the oven to 400°F/200°C.

2 Bring a large pan of water to a boil, add the leeks, and cook for 2 minutes. Add the butternut squash and cook for an additional 2 minutes. Drain in a colander. Mix the curry paste with the oil in a large bowl. Toss the leeks and butternut squash in the mixture to coat thoroughly.

3 Transfer the leeks and squash to a nonstick cookie sheet and roast in the preheated oven for 10 minutes, or until golden brown. Add the tomatoes and roast for an additional 5 minutes. Meanwhile, bring a large, heavy-bottom pan of lightly salted water to a boil. Add the pasta, return to a boil, and cook for 8–10 minutes, or until tender but still firm to the bite. Drain well. Put the white sauce into a large pan and warm over low heat. Add the leeks, squash, tomatoes, and cilantro and stir in the pasta. Serve immediately.

Step 1

Step 2

Step 3

penne with asparagus & gorgonzola

SERVES 4

1 lb/450 g asparagus tips

olive oil

8 oz/225 g Gorgonzola cheese, crumbled

¾ cup heavy cream

9 oz/250 g dried penne

salt and pepper

1 Preheat the oven to 450°F/230°C. Place the asparagus tips in a single layer in a shallow, ovenproof dish. Sprinkle with a little olive oil. Season to taste with salt and pepper. Turn to coat in the oil and seasoning.

2 Roast in the preheated oven for 10–12 minutes, or until slightly browned and just tender. Set aside and keep warm.

3 Combine the crumbled cheese with the cream in a bowl. Season to taste with salt and pepper.

4 Bring a large, heavy-bottom pan of lightly salted water to a boil. Add the pasta, return to a boil, and cook for 8–10 minutes, or until tender but still firm to the bite. Drain and transfer to a warmed serving dish.

5 Immediately add the asparagus and the cheese mixture to the pasta. Toss well, until the cheese has melted and the pasta is coated with the sauce. Serve immediately.

spaghetti alla norma

SERVES 4

¾ cup olive oil

8 plum tomatoes, peeled and chopped

1 garlic clove, chopped

¾ eggplant, diced

14 oz/400 g dried spaghetti

½ bunch fresh basil, torn

1⅓ cups freshly grated Romano cheese

salt and pepper

1 Heat 4 tablespoons of the oil in a large pan. Add the tomatoes and garlic, season to taste with salt and pepper, cover, and cook over low heat, stirring occasionally, for 25 minutes.

2 Meanwhile, heat the remaining oil in a heavy skillet. Add the eggplant and cook, stirring occasionally, for 5 minutes, until evenly golden brown. Remove with a slotted spoon and drain on paper towels.

3 Bring a large, heavy-bottom pan of lightly salted water to a boil. Add the pasta, return to a boil, and cook for 8–10 minutes, or until tender but still firm to the bite.

4 Meanwhile, stir the drained eggplant into the pan of tomatoes. Taste and adjust the seasoning, if necessary.

5 Drain the pasta and place in a warmed serving dish. Add the tomato and eggplant mixture, basil, and half of the Romano cheese. Toss well, sprinkle with the remaining cheese, and serve immediately.

fettuccine with peppers & olives

SERVES 4

⅓ **cup olive oil**

1 onion, finely chopped

1 cup black olives, pitted and coarsely chopped

14 oz/400 g of canned chopped tomatoes

2 red, yellow, or orange bell peppers, seeded and cut into thin strips

12 oz/350 g dried fettuccine

salt and pepper

shavings of Romano cheese, to serve

1 Heat the oil in a large, heavy-bottom pan. Add the onion and cook over low heat, stirring occasionally, for 5 minutes, or until softened. Add the olives, tomatoes, and bell peppers, and season to taste with salt and pepper. Cover and let simmer gently over very low heat, stirring occasionally, for 35 minutes.

2 Meanwhile, bring a large, heavy-bottom pan of lightly salted water to a boil. Add the pasta, return to a boil, and cook for 8–10 minutes, or until tender but still firm to the bite. Drain the pasta and transfer to a warmed serving dish.

3 Spoon the sauce onto the pasta and toss well. Sprinkle generously with the Romano cheese and serve immediately.

conchiglie with marinated artichoke

SERVES 4

10 oz/280 g bottled marinated artichoke hearts

3 tbsp olive oil

1 onion, finely chopped

3 garlic cloves, crushed

1 tsp dried oregano

¼ tsp dried chile flakes

14 oz/400 g of canned chopped tomatoes

12 oz/350 g dried conchiglie (shells)

4 tsp freshly grated Parmesan-style vegetarian cheese

3 tbsp chopped fresh flat-leaf parsley

salt and pepper

1 Drain the artichoke hearts, reserving the marinade. Heat the oil in a large, deep skillet over medium heat. Add the onion and fry for 5 minutes, or until translucent. Add the garlic, oregano, chile flakes, and the reserved artichoke marinade. Cook for an additional 5 minutes.

2 Stir in the tomatoes. Bring to a boil, then simmer over medium–low heat for 30 minutes. Season to taste with salt and pepper.

3 Bring a large, heavy-bottom pan of lightly salted water to a boil. Add the pasta, return to a boil, and cook for 8–10 minutes, or until tender but still firm to the bite. Drain and transfer to a warmed serving dish.

4 Add the artichokes, cheese, and parsley to the sauce. Cook for a few minutes until heated through. Pour the sauce over the top of the pasta, toss well to mix, and serve immediately.

Step 1

Step 2

Step 4

tagliatelle with garlic crumbs

SERVES 4

6 cups fresh white breadcrumbs

4 tbsp finely chopped fresh flat-leaf parsley

1 tbsp snipped fresh chives

2 tbsp finely chopped fresh marjoram

3 tbsp olive oil, plus extra to serve

3–4 garlic cloves, finely chopped

½ cup pine nuts

1 lb/450 g dried tagliatelle

salt and pepper

½ cup freshly grated Romano cheese, to serve

1 Mix the breadcrumbs, parsley, chives, and marjoram together in a small bowl. Heat the oil in a large, heavy-bottom skillet. Add the breadcrumb mixture and the garlic and pine nuts, season to taste with salt and pepper, and cook over low heat, stirring continuously, for 5 minutes, or until the breadcrumbs become golden, but not crisp. Remove the skillet from the heat and cover to keep warm until needed.

2 Bring a large, heavy-bottom pan of lightly salted water to a boil. Add the pasta, return to a boil, and cook for 8–10 minutes, or until tender but still firm to the bite.

3 Drain the pasta and transfer to a warmed serving dish. Drizzle with oil to taste and toss to mix. Add the garlic breadcrumbs and toss again. Serve immediately with the Romano cheese.

spaghetti with tomato & basil

SERVES 4

5 tbsp extra virgin olive oil

1 onion, finely chopped

1 lb 12 oz/800 g of canned chopped tomatoes

4 garlic cloves, cut into quarters

1 lb/450 g dried spaghetti

large handful fresh basil leaves, shredded

salt and pepper

shavings of fresh Parmesan-style vegetarian cheese, to serve

1 Heat the oil in a large pan over medium heat. Add the onion and cook gently for 5 minutes, or until softened. Add the tomatoes and garlic. Bring to a boil, then simmer over medium–low heat for 25–30 minutes, or until the oil separates from the tomato. Season to taste with salt and pepper.

2 Bring a large, heavy-bottom pan of lightly salted water to a boil. Add the pasta, return to a boil, and cook for 8–10 minutes, or until tender but still firm to the bite. Drain and transfer to a warmed serving dish.

3 Pour the sauce over the top of the pasta. Add the basil and toss well to mix. Serve with the cheese.

creamy pappardelle & broccoli

SERVES 4

4 tbsp butter

**1 large onion,
finely chopped**

**¾ bunch broccoli, broken
into florets**

**1 lb/450 g dried
pappardelle**

½ cup vegetable stock

1 tbsp all-purpose flour

½ cup light cream

**2 oz/55 g mozzarella
cheese, diced**

freshly grated nutmeg

salt and white pepper

**fresh apple slices,
to garnish**

1 Melt 2 tablespoons of the butter in a large pan over medium heat. Add the onion and cook for 4 minutes.

2 Add the broccoli and pasta to the pan and cook, stirring continuously, for 2 minutes. Add the stock, return to a boil, and cook for 8–10 minutes. Season well with salt and white pepper.

3 Meanwhile, melt the remaining butter in a pan over medium heat. Sprinkle with the flour and cook, stirring continuously, for 2 minutes. Gradually stir in the cream and bring to a simmer, but do not boil. Add the mozzarella cheese and season to taste with salt and a little freshly grated nutmeg.

4 Drain the pasta and broccoli mixture and return to the pan. Pour in the cheese sauce and cook, stirring occasionally, for about 2 minutes. Transfer the pasta and broccoli mixture to warmed serving dishes and garnish with a few slices of apple. Serve immediately.

spicy eggplant, chickpea & cilantro penne

SERVES 4

large pinch of saffron threads

2 cups hot vegetable stock

2 tbsp olive oil

1 large onion, coarsely chopped

1 tsp cumin seeds, crushed

¾ eggplant, diced

1 large red bell pepper, seeded and chopped

14 oz/400 g of canned chopped tomatoes

1 tsp ground cinnamon

14 sprigs cilantro, leaves and stems, separated and coarsely chopped

14 oz/400 g of canned chickpeas, drained and rinsed

10 oz/280 g dried penne

salt and pepper

harissa or chili sauce, to serve (optional)

1 Toast the saffron threads in a dry skillet set over medium heat for 20–30 seconds, just until they begin to give off their aroma. Put into a small bowl and crumble with your fingers. Add 2 tablespoons of the hot stock and set aside.

2 Heat the oil in a large pan. Add the onion and cook for 5–6 minutes, or until golden brown. Add the cumin and cook for an additional 20–30 seconds, then stir in the eggplant, bell pepper, tomatoes, cinnamon, cilantro stems, saffron liquid, and remaining stock. Cover and simmer for 20 minutes.

3 Add the chickpeas to the pan and season to taste with salt and pepper. Simmer for 5 minutes more, removing the lid to reduce and thicken the sauce, if necessary.

4 Bring a large, heavy-bottom pan of lightly salted water to a boil. Add the pasta, return to a boil, and cook for 8–10 minutes, or until tender but still firm to the bite. Drain and transfer to a warmed serving bowl. Add the sauce and half of the cilantro leaves, then toss. Garnish with the remaining cilantro and serve immediately with the harissa or chili sauce, if a more spicy taste is desired.

Step 1

Step 2

Step 3

rigatoni with bell peppers & goat cheese

SERVES 4

2 tbsp olive oil

1 tbsp butter

1 small onion, finely chopped

4 bell peppers, yellow and red, seeded and cut into ¾-inch/2-cm squares

3 garlic cloves, thinly sliced

1 lb/450 g dried rigatoni (pasta tubes)

4½ oz/125 g goat cheese, crumbled

15 fresh basil leaves, shredded

10 black olives, pitted and sliced

salt and pepper

1 Heat the oil and butter in a large skillet over medium heat. Add the onion and cook until softened. Raise the heat to medium–high and add the bell peppers and garlic. Cook for 12–15 minutes, stirring continuously, or until the peppers are tender but not mushy. Season to taste with salt and pepper. Remove from the heat.

2 Bring a large, heavy-bottom pan of lightly salted water to a boil. Add the pasta, return to a boil, and cook for 8–10 minutes, or until tender but still firm to the bite. Drain and transfer to a warmed serving dish. Add the goat cheese and toss to mix.

3 Briefly reheat the onion and pepper mixture. Add the basil and olives. Pour over the top of the pasta and toss well to mix. Serve immediately.

fusilli with zucchini & lemon

SERVES 4

6 tbsp olive oil

1 small onion, very thinly sliced

2 garlic cloves, very finely chopped

2 tbsp chopped fresh rosemary

1 tbsp chopped fresh flat-leaf parsley

4 small zucchini, cut into 1½-inch/4-cm lengths

finely grated rind of 1 lemon

1 lb/450 g dried fusilli

salt and pepper

freshly grated Parmesan-style vegetarian cheese, to serve

1 Heat the oil in a large skillet over medium–low heat. Add the onion and cook gently, stirring occasionally, for about 10 minutes, or until golden.

2 Raise the heat to medium–high. Add the garlic, rosemary, and parsley. Cook for a few seconds, stirring continuously.

3 Add the zucchini and lemon rind. Cook for 5–7 minutes, stirring occasionally, or until the zucchini are just tender. Season to taste with salt and pepper. Remove from the heat.

4 Bring a large, heavy-bottom pan of lightly salted water to a boil. Add the pasta, return to a boil, and cook for 8–10 minutes, or until tender but still firm to the bite. Drain and transfer to a warmed serving dish.

5 Briefly reheat the zucchini sauce. Pour over the top of the pasta and toss well to mix. Sprinkle with the cheese and serve immediately.

penne with mixed beans

SERVES 4

1 tbsp olive oil

1 onion, chopped

1 garlic clove, finely chopped

1 carrot, finely chopped

1 celery stalk, finely chopped

1¾ cups mixed canned beans, such as cannellini beans, chickpeas, and northern beans

1 cup tomato puree

1 tbsp chopped fresh chervil, plus extra leaves to garnish

12 oz/350 g dried penne

salt and pepper

1 Heat the oil in a large, heavy-bottom skillet. Add the onion, garlic, carrot, and celery, and cook over low heat, stirring occasionally, for 5 minutes, or until the onion has softened.

2 Add the mixed beans, tomato puree, and chopped chervil to the skillet and season the mixture to taste with salt and pepper. Cover and simmer gently for 15 minutes.

3 Meanwhile, bring a large, heavy-bottom pan of lightly salted water to a boil. Add the pasta, return to a boil, and cook for 8–10 minutes, or until tender but still firm to the bite. Drain the pasta and transfer to a warmed serving dish. Add the mixed bean sauce, toss well, and serve immediately, garnished with extra chervil.

ziti with arugula

SERVES 4

**12 oz/350 g dried ziti,
broken into 1½-inch/
4-cm lengths**

5 tbsp extra virgin olive oil

**2 garlic cloves,
lightly crushed**

3½ cups arugula

**2 fresh red chiles,
thickly sliced**

**fresh red chile flowers,
to garnish**

**freshly grated Romano
cheese, to serve**

salt

1 Bring a large, heavy-bottom pan of lightly salted water to a boil. Add the pasta, return to a boil, and cook for 8–10 minutes, or until tender but still firm to the bite.

2 Meanwhile, heat the olive oil in a large, heavy-bottom skillet. Add the garlic, arugula, and sliced chiles and fry for 5 minutes, or until the arugula has wilted.

3 Stir 2 tablespoons of the pasta cooking water into the arugula mixture, then drain the pasta and add to the skillet. Cook, stirring frequently, for 2 minutes, then transfer to a warmed serving dish. Remove and discard the garlic cloves and chiles, garnish with red chile flowers, and serve immediately with the Romano cheese.

Step 2

Step 3

Step 3

tagliatelle with walnuts

SERVES 4

½ cup fresh white breadcrumbs

3 cups walnut pieces

2 garlic cloves, finely chopped

4 tbsp milk

4 tbsp olive oil

½ cup cream cheese

⅔ cup light cream

12 oz/350 g dried tagliatelle

salt and pepper

sprigs of fresh flat-leaf parsley, to garnish

1 Place the breadcrumbs, walnuts, garlic, milk, oil, and cream cheese in a large mortar and grind to a smooth paste with a pestle. Alternatively, place the ingredients in a food processor and process until smooth. Stir in the cream to give a thick sauce consistency and season to taste with salt and pepper. Set aside.

2 Bring a large, heavy-bottom pan of lightly salted water to a boil. Add the pasta, return to a boil, and cook for 8–10 minutes, or until tender but still firm to the bite.

3 Drain the pasta and transfer to a warmed serving dish. Add the walnut sauce and toss thoroughly to coat. Garnish with parsley and serve immediately.

fusilli with ricotta, mint & garlic

SERVES 4

10½ oz/300 g dried fusilli

½ cup ricotta cheese

1–2 roasted garlic cloves from a jar, finely chopped

⅔ cup heavy cream

1 tbsp chopped fresh mint, plus extra sprigs to garnish

salt and pepper

1 Bring a large, heavy-bottom pan of lightly salted water to a boil. Add the pasta, return to a boil, and cook for 8–10 minutes, or until tender but still firm to the bite.

2 Beat the ricotta, garlic, cream, and chopped mint together in a bowl until smooth.

3 Drain the cooked pasta, then return to the pan. Pour in the cheese mixture and toss together. Season to taste with pepper and serve immediately, garnished with the mint sprigs.

tagliatelle with wild mushrooms & mascarpone

SERVES 4

1 lb/450 g dried tagliatelle

4 tbsp butter

1 garlic clove, finely chopped

8 oz/225 g mixed wild mushrooms, halved

generous 1 cup mascarpone cheese

2 tbsp milk

1 tsp chopped fresh sage, plus extra leaves to garnish

salt and pepper

freshly grated Parmesan-style vegetarian cheese, to serve

1 Bring a large, heavy-bottom pan of lightly salted water to a boil. Add the pasta, return to a boil, and cook for 8–10 minutes, or until tender but still firm to the bite.

2 Meanwhile, melt the butter in a separate large pan. Add the garlic and mushrooms and cook for 3–4 minutes.

3 Reduce the heat and stir in the mascarpone cheese, milk, and sage. Season to taste with salt and pepper.

4 Drain the pasta thoroughly and add to the mushroom sauce. Toss until the pasta is well coated with the sauce. Transfer to warmed dishes and serve immediately with the cheese.

chile broccoli pasta

SERVES 4

8 oz/225 g dried penne or macaroni

2 fresh red chiles, seeded

⅓ bunch broccoli, cut into florets

¼ cup extra virgin olive oil

2 large garlic cloves, crushed

8 cherry tomatoes

handful of fresh basil leaves, to garnish

salt

1 Bring a large, heavy-bottom pan of lightly salted water to a boil. Add the pasta, return to a boil, and cook for 8–10 minutes, or until tender but still firm to the bite. Drain the pasta, refresh under cold running water, and drain again. Set aside.

2 Cut the chiles into small cubes. Bring a pan of salted water to a boil, add the broccoli, and cook for 5 minutes. Drain, refresh under cold running water, and drain again.

3 Heat the oil in the pan that the pasta was cooked in over high heat. Add the garlic, chopped chiles, and tomatoes, and cook, stirring continuously, for 1 minute.

4 Add the broccoli and mix well. Cook for 2 minutes, stirring, to heat through. Add the pasta and mix well again. Cook for an additional minute. Transfer the pasta to a large, warmed serving bowl and serve garnished with basil leaves.

Step 2

Step 2

Step 4

pappardelle with pumpkin sauce

SERVES 4

4 tbsp butter

6 shallots, very finely chopped

⅓ pumpkin (about 1 lb 12 oz/800 g), peeled, seeded, and cut into pieces

pinch of freshly grated nutmeg

¾ cup light cream

4 tbsp freshly grated Parmesan-style vegetarian cheese, plus extra to serve

2 tbsp chopped fresh flat-leaf parsley

12 oz/350 g dried pappardelle

salt

1 Melt the butter in a large, heavy-bottom pan. Add the shallots, sprinkle with a little salt, cover, and cook over very low heat, stirring occasionally, for 30 minutes.

2 Add the pumpkin pieces and season with the nutmeg. Cover and cook over very low heat, stirring occasionally, for 40 minutes, or until the pumpkin is pulpy. Stir in the cream, cheese, and parsley, and remove the pan from the heat.

3 Meanwhile, bring a large, heavy-bottom pan of lightly salted water to a boil. Add the pasta, return to a boil, and cook for 8–10 minutes, or until tender but still firm to the bite. Drain, reserving 2–3 tablespoons of the cooking water.

4 Add the pasta to the pumpkin mixture and stir in the reserved cooking water if the mixture seems too thick. Cook, stirring continuously, for 1 minute, then transfer to a warmed serving dish and serve immediately with extra grated cheese.

linguine with garlic & bell peppers

SERVES 4

6 large garlic cloves, unpeeled

14 oz/400 g bottled roasted red bell peppers, drained and sliced

7 oz/200 g of canned chopped tomatoes

3 tbsp olive oil

¼ tsp dried chile flakes

1 tsp chopped fresh oregano or thyme, plus extra sprigs to garnish

12 oz/350 g dried linguine

salt and pepper

1 Preheat the oven to 400°F/200°C. Place the unpeeled garlic cloves in a shallow, ovenproof dish. Roast in the preheated oven for 7–10 minutes, or until the garlic cloves feel soft.

2 Put the bell peppers, tomatoes, and oil in a food processor or blender, then process until pureed. Squeeze the garlic flesh into the puree. Add the chile flakes and oregano. Season to taste with salt and pepper. Blend again, then scrape into a pan and set aside.

3 Bring a large, heavy-bottom pan of lightly salted water to a boil. Add the pasta, return to a boil, and cook for 8–10 minutes, or until tender but still firm to the bite. Drain and transfer to a warmed serving dish.

4 Reheat the sauce and pour over the top of the pasta. Toss well to mix, garnish with oregano sprigs, and serve immediately.

fettuccine with garlic, tomatoes & olives

SERVES 4

4 plum tomatoes, peeled, seeded, and chopped

4 garlic cloves, finely chopped

8 black olives, pitted and finely chopped

1 red chile, seeded and finely chopped

2 tbsp chopped fresh flat-leaf parsley

2 tbsp extra virgin olive oil

1 tbsp lemon juice

10 oz/280 g dried fettuccine

salt and pepper

1 Place the tomatoes in a large, nonmetallic strainer set over a bowl. Cover and set aside in the refrigerator for 30 minutes.

2 Combine the garlic, olives, chile, parsley, oil, and lemon juice in a separate bowl. Season to taste with salt and pepper. Cover and set aside in the refrigerator until required.

3 Add the tomatoes to the garlic mixture, discarding the drained juice.

4 Bring a large, heavy-bottom pan of lightly salted water to a boil. Add the pasta, return to a boil, and cook for 8–10 minutes, or until tender but still firm to the bite. Drain, then turn into a warmed serving bowl. Add the garlic and tomato mixture and toss well. Serve immediately.

penne with creamy mushrooms

SERVES 4

4 tbsp butter

1 tbsp olive oil

6 shallots, sliced

1 lb/450 g cremini mushrooms, sliced

1 tsp all-purpose flour

⅔ cup heavy cream

2 tbsp port

¾ cup drained and chopped sun-dried tomatoes in oil

pinch of freshly grated nutmeg

12 oz/350 g dried penne

salt and pepper

2 tbsp chopped fresh flat-leaf parsley, to garnish

1 Melt the butter with the olive oil in a large, heavy-bottom skillet. Add the shallots and cook over low heat, stirring occasionally, for 4–5 minutes, or until softened. Add the mushrooms and cook over low heat for an additional 2 minutes. Season to taste with salt and pepper, sprinkle in the flour, and cook, stirring continuously, for 1 minute.

2 Remove the skillet from the heat and gradually stir in the cream and port. Return to the heat, add the sun-dried tomatoes and grated nutmeg, and cook over low heat, stirring occasionally, for 8 minutes.

3 Meanwhile, bring a large, heavy-bottom pan of lightly salted water to a boil. Add the pasta, return to a boil, and cook for 8–10 minutes, or until tender but still firm to the bite. Drain the pasta well and add to the mushroom sauce. Cook for 3 minutes, then transfer to a warmed serving dish. Garnish with the chopped parsley and serve immediately.

VARIATION

Omit the sun-dried tomatoes and add 3 garlic cloves, finely chopped, with the shallots, plus 1 teaspoon each of chopped fresh rosemary and oregano.